I AM A PRISONER OF HOPE

Samuel Ole Lotegeluaki, Ph.D

Front cover design by Jonathan Lotegeluaki.
ISBN: 979-8-35091-037-7 paperback
ISBN: 979-8-35091-038-4 ebook

ACKNOWLEDGEMENTS

I owe my sincere and deep appreciation for inspiring my thoughts in this book to all members of my family, especially to my dear, loving wife Janet, whose gentle and loving advice became a source of my strength.

Lastly, I am eternally indebted to my late parents, whose daily prayers inspired me to keep hope alive. Equally, I stand indebted to my late, beloved in-laws, Mr. and Mrs. Wallace Aarsvold, for their love and compassion.

CONTENTS

INTRODUCTION

A few years ago, I was standing in a rather long line to order a cup of "chai" at a Starbuck's café within a Target Store in St. Paul. The waiting seemed to be a bit longer, probably because those ahead of me ordered several items for their friends or colleagues. Two gentlemen ahead of me were conversing in a language which was not English. I was listening and trying to figure out what country they originally came from. They were conversing and laughing, and once in a while the gentleman in front of me would turn around and smile at me, saying "this waiting is going on forever," and then he would turn away and continue a conversation with his friend. I waited for a while; when he stopped talking, I asked him whether he stopped at this place often. He responded: "Oh yes, we come here during our breaks. We work two blocks away from here." I said to him, "You remind me of some people I grew up with in Africa." And then he asked, "Where was your home?" When I told them that I am a Maasai from Tanzania, they both turned to me with big smiles on their faces, and asked me if I spoke Kiswahili. They had originally come from Somali but had learned Kiswahili when they were war refugees in Kenya. Quickly, it went from strangers to friends. We exchanged phone numbers before we ever got our "chai". Originally, I had stood in a line to get my one cup of chai, and at the end I left with my chai and a heart-warming story of two friendly young persons. I walked back to my office smiling, because I made two friends without much effort at all. Yes, you can say I took a risk; however. it was worth taking. I want to take a risk now and introduce myself to you as well.

As you may have already guessed, I live in Minnesota, even though I was born and raised in Tanzania (then Tanganyika). Minnesota, which is known for her very cold winters and very warm summers, is now my adopted home. My wife and I live a few miles away from the Twin Cities, very much out in the country. Our town is very small, and away from busy highways. I tend to enjoy less noisy nights, and the sight of cattle alongside the country road is an added bonus for me. Make no mistake, driving on narrow country roads during the winter can be punishing; however, I would not give up my life in the country just to have the convenient services of a bigger city. I just do not enjoy spending my life in any larger city. To give you a clue why I feel the way I do, we once lived in one of the large cities in the Midwest for thirty years. We raised our children in that city, and I am glad we had a chance to do so. Truthfully, living in that city did help our children to value diversity; therefore, there are no regrets at all. In Tanzania, our family (as I was growing up) did not live close to any town, let alone a city. Those years Maasai did not see the value of cities or towns. The city of Arusha was comprised of a few government buildings in the 1940s. There were no roads or streets that you find today. My childhood environment shaped me, which means I tend to prefer the countryside before I can think of a city. Put it this way: my uneasiness with big cities is partly cultural and socialization. Coming from a nomadic tribe, I find myself listening more than talking, and adopting my surroundings incrementally. Big cities tend to have so much activity going on continuously, that a person like me has a very difficult time pondering and reflecting on events of the day.

When we moved to this small town, we knew very well it was going to be a long commute to St. Paul where we both worked. We were fortunate to find a house with a back yard bordered by a ravine with beautiful trees. I like trees, I like to garden, and I have a passion for flowers. The house has a deck on the back facing the ravine dressed with tall trees lavishly dancing as the gentle wind combs through the pretty green branches. Every working day I could not wait to get home, just to have a few minutes or hours of sitting and watching wildlife, especially colorful birds feeding in our back-yard. Even though it might sound very strange to some people, one of the reasons I prefer country over towns or cities, is the fact that, often, I find myself drifting or rather sliding into the sea of meditation where logic surrenders its dominion. In moments like that, I immerse into a sea of tranquility, and appreciation of a clear view of a rose garden in the middle of a screeching hurricane. Beneath my warrior-like personality, there dwells a gentle and compassionate baby boy. Somebody once said, "A great man is he who has not lost the heart of a child" (Mencius). In the midst of my philosophical reasoning, there lies a simplistic and childlike hypothesis of how to walk the tight rope of life. As I swim in a pool of my unconsciousness, I realize my inability to appreciate tomorrow, and only in today can I make sense of yesterday.

CHAPTER ONE:
A GLOBAL CANOPY

One summer night, I stepped out to our deck. It was a very clear night. As I looked up, no cloud in sight, all I could see was a beautiful dome of stars. I got excited about that and pulled up a chair and sat down; looking up, I could see the whole dome full of stars glittering as if they were dancing. That sight took me back to my birth place. It was a bit late in the night, which explains why the neighbors' lights were turned off. Other than sounds of frogs, crickets, and buzzing bugs, it was amazingly quiet, and I stayed still looking at all those stars. I could hear my heart-beats, the sounds of bugs, and strange creatures in the ravine communicating uniquely. The more I drifted into this awesome feeling and awareness of presence inside this magnificent dome which is gloriously decorated by numberless stars, the more I re-entered my childhood. As a child, I grew up in an environment where people did not build rectangular buildings, but rather huts, just big enough to accommodate mothers and their children. Men, or rather grown up male adults, slept in their own separate huts, mostly closer to the cattle, goats and sheep. I began visualizing my mother's hut, and how all of us (eight children) shared our little sleeping spots. As my mother kept the fire going as means of warming the hut (May, June and July were always cold), I remembered looking at the beams (branches) which held the hut together at the very peak. Those beams were tied together, resting on a central pole of the hut itself. Under such a canopy, we did not escape the typical sibling squabbles; however, we knew that we all belonged there despite our differences. This night, I felt at peace again just like I did in my mother's hut. I lost track of time, because by the time I regained awareness, my neck was hurting from looking up for a long time without moving a muscle, which gave the mosquitoes an opportunity to bite me that night. The experience of that night did certainly change my world view. I gained a feeling of being in a confined place and yet free to choose. Seriously, there are no words to express what actually changed in me that night. To this very day I feel free and simultaneously feel indebted and owing this world something. I can no longer step on that deck without thinking of the canopy which my mother's hut symbolized.

Day and night I am reminded of the fact that we as human beings, regardless of culture, language, religion, gender, skin color or social economic status, are all under God's huge canopy, and we are convincingly related. You may not look exactly like me, but rest assured, we are not just related, but more importantly, we are siblings. Do not be fooled by the looks, for I come from a family of eight, yet we did not look exactly alike. Inside this global canopy (metaphorically speaking) one may encounter a fellow human being whose manners or behavior seem unconventional. At this point you (or anyone else) need to remind yourself that the canopy I am talking about is planet earth, a place we all call home. None of us can claim the absolute ownership of this global canopy. Yes, you or I may indulge the ego by talking, thinking, and acting as if we have the absolute ownership of the place we are standing on, or of what we possess. However, when you stop and think of all that you have accumulated since birth, you might feel very good or disappointed, depending on your stage in life. Regardless of the outcome of your feelings, the next logical question should be: how much did you own at birth? Subsequently, as you look around very carefully, do you see those people who first planned and built our roads and cities we now reside in and proudly call our own? What happened to the people who had the wealth of this country in their hands? How much did they take with them? Don't you think that generally we waste precious time squabbling over minor things in life? Pushing away and suppressing other people because they happened to think differently, or came from places we never heard of before? Or mistreating those who happened to be of the opposite gender? My dear friends, dismissing the importance and the dignity of another person due to unfamiliarity of that particular person, is nothing but a short-lived comfort of narrow-mindedness, which we all know will never be a solution to the racism, prejudice, and discrimination which in the last few years have gained a hurricane strength category.

At this point I am reminded of a certain incident in California some years back, when a young distressed black American (Rodney King), while experiencing emotional and physical pain from the heavy handedness of the Police, shouted, "CAN WE ALL GET ALONG?" I heard the question, and probably many of you or some of your friends heard that question too, or you probably read it in your local newspaper. That question was uttered by a hurting person, and to this day it still glitters in my mind. The question was not sophisticated; nonetheless, it caught my attention. To be blunt, this is the most difficult question we will ever encounter as citizens of planet earth. In this canopy (earth), seeing and hearing what we do to other human beings could be discouraging. Rational human beings cannot ignore this fundamental question because it reminds all of us that we share the "earth" we call home. The logical answer to Rodney King's question is not only "Yes" but rather, "WE MUST!" Commonsense dictates that, unless we live and get along as people, as Americans or just as human beings regardless of country of origin, culture, gender, religion, age, social economic status or skin color, we will surely perish together. Our choices are limited. We cannot just take off and make a home in some other places such as Mars or even the moon. Probably in a few years we might have the ability and knowledge to build cities on Mars or other places in our solar system. But until that time, we cannot run away from each other. The world's population is growing much faster, and resources are diminishing. That being the case, I predict that conflicts between nations over water resources, and basic life essentials, will be the precursor of major global conflicts.

In my mind, the aforementioned question did not suggest or imply assimilation. The question called for recognition and respect for individuality, drawing its meaning from the acknowledgement of what is known as "related-ness". Being an individual does not eliminate relatedness. I seriously think a human psyche is not entirely curved into itself; it relates to the outside world. For instance, it perceives, encodes, interprets and then determines the course of action. It is also true that human beings do not thrive in isolation. My point is: the true meaning of "individuality" is not divorced from the meaning of "group".

While we know that it is absolutely possible for individuals to form a group, we also know that group members (individuals) are not stripped of their personal identities. In spite of their different talents or likes and dislikes, they can still be productive members of the group. However, there are those who interpret differences or dissimilarities negatively. It makes one wonder if these people were ever able to share their toys with other children as they were growing up. They grew up believing they had the "ultimate truth" in their hands. Consequently, they turn out to be bullies and egocentric individuals. Such people are closed minded, and it is very difficult to convince them that "goodness" can be experienced anywhere in the world. From my perspective, the need to get along is larger than the state of California. The need to get along encompasses not only Americans, regardless of economic status, skin color, gender, religious beliefs, citizenship, age, or political beliefs. We all belong to one race, and that is the "human race". Getting along is not and should not be a choice, but rather a necessity. Those who belong to the human race MUST get along. Again, I am not implying that there will come a time where all people in the world will have a single opinion on certain things. I believe that would be humanly impossible because our upbringing, cultures, languages, geographical differences and religious beliefs will always remain diversified; yet we need to remind ourselves that "diversity" does not breed strife.

Let me ask you: when do you help others? I ask you this question because I was asked this question many times, not only by my students over the years, but also by colleagues. This question is relevant to me because it always reminds me of my father's statement: "you are never done until your neighbor is done." As a little boy I had a difficult time understanding the significance of that statement, and yet it remained in my head all these years. His statement impacted my behavior in regard to anyone who happened to be my neighbor everywhere I went. The impact of that statement, gave me (and still does) a feeling of wanting to help a neighbor whether I am asked or not. In this country I found out that such a feeling can sometimes be misunderstood. Yet there is a little voice in my head, which does not give me peace of mind if I encounter someone who seems to need help and I do not help. I seem to have no peace of mind until I offer my help. I have to admit, it is not a bad thing to help someone else, but one needs to be careful because in some cultures, offering help without being asked can be interpreted as rude and invasive. Therefore, now I hesitate to offer my help even when I think it is needed.

Some of you might have heard or read a story about a young lady who was attacked by a rapist as she returned to her apartment in the middle of the night. Her screams of terror and pleas for help, saying, "Oh my God, he stabbed me!" aroused 38 of her neighbors. Many came to their windows and watched while she struggled to escape her attacker. You should know that not until the attacker departed, did anyone decide to call the police, and by that time she was dead. If I was sharing this story with you in person, and somehow asked you, "When would you feel comfortable helping a person in trouble?" I suspect some of you would probably say something like: usually you would help a friend, a relative, a person asking for help, a non-threatening person or a person who is familiar to you. Or you can offer your help to an older person or a child which shows that you are kind and a very caring person. Okay, let us look into another incident which took place in one of our large cities a few years back. A middle-aged lady, while shopping for Christmas, tripped and broke her leg. Dazed and in sharp pain, she pleaded for help. For about 49 minutes, Christmas shoppers just walked around her, and finally a cab-driver stopped to help and took her to the hospital.

So, my question to you is brief and clear: WHEN DO YOU HELP OTHERS? Or for some of us who are little older, I would like to ask this general question which is: "why is it that not many good-hearted Germans endangered their lives by taking to the streets to rescue Jews and many other people who did not fit Hitler's definition of a "good German"? Today we may look at these things and say how awful these people were; we look at ourselves and say we would not have just stood by and done nothing, because we are religious. We would have taken to the streets and denounced that brutal policy. Some of us who are self-righteous would have an "us" vs "them" mentality. I am reminded of the parable of the Good Samaritan as recorded in the Bible (Luke 10: 30-35). Being Christian or not, this parable illustrates pure altruism. Remember, altruism is selfishness in reverse. Filled with compassion, the man in the parable gave a total stranger time, energy, and money while expecting neither repayment nor appreciation. Some people might suggest that we should not take one passage of the Bible and draw a conclusion. Perhaps that is a helpful suggestion; however, what other conclusion can you draw from this parable? There are those of us who want to cook up justification, real or not, so we can live with ourselves. We do not want to feel uncomfortable in our beliefs, therefore we read the Bible and understand it from our own perspectives. For instance, when we run into a passage in which Jesus said, "give without expecting anything in return," we quickly search for an interpretation which will not trigger guilt.

Social psychologists have found that in many cases, the act of helping increases among people who are feeling guilty. Helping provides a way to relieve the guilt or restore self- image. Helping also increases when a person is in a good mood, and finally social psychologists have discovered that helping increases among people who are deeply religious. With the importance of these findings, we should also understand that circumstances do play a role in when to help. Researchers found that the odds of our helping someone increases when: we are not hurried; the victim appears to need and deserve help; the victim is similar to ourselves; we are in a small town or rural area; or there are few other bystanders.

So why do you want to help other people? First, what motivates altruism? There is a possibility that we help after doing a cost-benefit analysis, and this is known as "social exchange theory". As part of an exchange of benefits, helpers aim to maximize their rewards and minimize their costs. For instance, when donating blood, one usually weighs the cost (the inconvenience and discomfort) against the benefit (the social approval and noble feeling). If the anticipated rewards exceed the costs, we usually help. You might object that social exchange theory takes the selflessness out of altruism. It seems to imply that a helpful act is never genuinely altruistic; we merely call it "altruistic" when the rewards are inconspicuous. If we know people are helping only to alleviate guilt or gain social approval, we hardly credit them for a good deed. We laud people for their altruism only when we can't otherwise explain it.

From babyhood onward, people sometimes exhibit a natural empathy, by feeling stress when seeing others in distress and relief when their suffering ends. Loving parents (unlike child abusers and other perpetrators) suffer when their children suffer and rejoice over their children's joy. Although some helpful acts are done to gain rewards or relieve guilt, experiments suggest that other helpful acts aim simply to increase another's welfare, producing satisfaction for oneself merely as a by-product. Social norms also motivate helping. They prescribe how we ought to behave. We learn the reciprocity norm—that we should return help to those who have helped us. Therefore, we expect that those who receive favors (gifts, invitations, help) should later return them. The reciprocity norm is qualified by our awareness that some people are incapable of reciprocal giving and receiving. Thus, we also feel a social responsibility norm that we should help those who really need it, without regard to future exchanges. This often reminds me of what Jesus said in regard to our attitude when it comes to helping others who are in need, those who are not strategically beneficial to us. Matthew 25: 42-46:

For I was hungry, and you gave me no food, I was thirsty and you gave me nothing to drink, I was a stranger and you did not welcome me, naked and you did not give me clothing, sick and in prison and you did not visit me . . . Then He will answer them, Truly I tell you, just as you did not do it to one of the least of these, you did not do it to me. And these will go away into eternal punishment, but the righteous into eternal life. (New Revised Standard Version, Holy Bible, XL Edition. *Matthew25: 42-46.* 1989, pp. 911).

How do we handle the words of Jesus to a young King as we read in Mark 10:17-23?

As he was setting out on a journey, a man ran up and knelt before him, and asked him, "Good Teacher, what must I do to inherit eternal life?" Jesus said to him, "Why do you call me good? No one is good but God alone. You know the commandments: You shall not murder; You shall not commit adultery; You shall not steal; You shall not bear false witness; You shall not defraud; Honor your father and mother." He said to him, "Teacher, I have kept all these since my youth." Jesus looked at him, loved him and said "You lack one thing, go sell what you own and give the money to the poor, and you will have treasure in heaven; then come and follow me". When he heard this, he was shocked and went away grieving, for he had many possessions. Then Jesus looked around and said to his disciples, "How hard it will be for those who have wealth to enter the kingdom of God" (New Revised Standard Version, Holy Bible, XL Edition. *Mark 10:17-23.* 1989, p. 928).

This young ruler was very sure he did everything necessary here on earth, so entering the Heavenly kingdom was a sure thing; however he wanted to check with Jesus if there is anything he was missing. Sadly, the response was, "go thy way, sell whatsoever you have, and give to the poor, and you shall have treasure in heaven: and come, take up the cross, and follow me". This young ruler was shocked and saddened by Christ's response. By the way, Christ did not say, this young, rich ruler cannot enter the kingdom of God, or that the list of things he had done so far were useless. Jesus loved him and what he had accomplished so far; however, he had to pass the final examination, that was: to sell whatsoever he had and give to the poor here on earth, for he will have treasure in heaven. In contemporary language one could say: you cannot have it both ways. You are at the cross-road; pick up the direction you believe is going to get you to your destination. Many people can relate to what the young ruler felt after his enthusiastic interview with Christ from which he got more than he bargained for. Probably some of us might create and make wonderful excuses for what we do or not do in some certain situations.

Justification has been used most of the time to silence the guilt for crafting and designing a "stratification society". More than any other time in the history of mankind, the ladder to basic survivability has become unimaginable. The gap between the "rich" and the "poor" in this century is astronomical, and I do not see a logical and peaceful way to narrow the gap between the very rich and very poor. In the heart of civilization and scientific discoveries, mankind is losing a "soul" and persistently curving inwardly, reminiscing the fetus stage which is no longer attainable. Many of us would like to remain as bystanders, or would like to play deaf and blind to all of the problems of our time. We do not even dare to speak up when governments, or dictators of the world, kill others and their citizens indiscriminately. We fear losing business with these dictators; or we keep our eyes closed and cover our ears when our own leaders separate hundreds of children from their parents, concurrently cheering and supporting groups which go out hunting to kill others for political reasons, or for their skin-color or gender. How do we dare point our fingers at Germans who covered their ears when Hitler was killing those who did not fit his definition of pure race? At the same time, our own generation dared to watch George Floyd pinned on the ground by a racist, and his cry for help was muted by personal fear. By the way, we became not only witnesses but in reality "paralyzed participants". A brutal crime was displayed in front of fellow citizens, and their rapid reactions were to turn on their cameras while a vicious brute continued to squeeze life out of another person. If you were there when an innocent person was being denied oxygen, in retrospect what would you have done to save his life in addition to turning on your camera on this brutal killer? Chances were, had you attempted to physically intervene or engage the "blood thirsty killer" we would have had more people dead on that spot. There would have been a big cry, that you were interfering with the law enforcement. Now we are beginning to understand why so many good and decent Germans were not able to confront Adolf Hitler. In a nutshell: you and I are not much different from those German citizens who witnessed the brutality and killing of innocent citizens by Adolf Hitler and did not speak up for the fear of their own lives. The killing of George Floyd evoked the memories of what Hitler did to many people. Just as the Jews did not have court hearings and juries to render a verdict, similarly George Floyd was tried and found guilty by a modern-day Hitler. George Floyd was never given an opportunity to tell his story, which means he was innocent until proven guilty. His killer became the judge and the executioner. According to the laws of this country, one is innocent until proven guilty. His killer did not have a case to convict him, therefore he silenced him forever. He did this in front of witnesses. Our silence and inaction come very close to the story of the man wounded by thieves as recorded in Luke 10:30-37:

> Jesus replied, a man was going down from Jerusalem to Jericho, and fell into the hands of robbers who stripped him, beat him, and went away leaving him half dead. Now by chance a priest was going down that road and when he

saw him, he passed by the other side. So likewise, a Levite, when he came to the place and saw him passed by on the other side. But a Samaritan while traveling came near him; and when he saw him, he was moved with pity. He went to him and bandaged his wounds, having poured oil and wine on them. Then he put him on his own animal, brought him to an inn, and took care of him. The next day he took out two denarii, gave them to the innkeeper, and said, "Take care of him, and when I come back, I will repay you whatever more you spend". Which of these three, do you think, was a good a neighbor of the man who fell into the hands of the robbers? He said, "The one who showed him mercy". Jesus said to him, "Go and do likewise". (New Revised Standard Version, Holy Bible, XL Edition. *Luke 10:30-37*. 1989, pp. 953-954).

Witnessing a brutal and senseless murder and taking no action to save life, puts you and me right back to the story in Luke 10: 30-37. We remove ourselves from the troubled areas of the world, and we claim that we cannot do anything as individuals; yet we forget this simple reality: that "group" is a byproduct of "individual". In other words, you cannot have "many" in absence of "one". As much as we wish, we cannot hide or run away from "I-ness" or "me-ness". I cannot hide in a group forever, because life calls for personal action. Many times, we forget that we share one earth, and if we stand by and play mute and deaf, we are indirectly encouraging and cheering the blood-thirsty brutal regimes. The point is, we can run away, and make wonderful excuses; but we cannot hide from the voice of God asking: WHERE IS YOUR BROTHER/SISTER? Those who claim to be religious, whether Christians, Muslims, or Hindu, should know that "faith" without good fruit is a dead "faith". If you are hanging on your faith as an identification card which differentiates you from other people, and yet you are not producing fruits of faith, I am inclined to say that something is missing in the whole process, namely: fruit of faith. Remember, "faith" is not barren. As much time as you spend praying and fasting, the gentle voice of God continues to be heard in your daily endeavor: "Where is your brother and where is your sister? What did you do to them?" That nagging voice of the Creator cannot be wished away or buried in the dirt or thrown away somewhere. It is constantly in your conscience, and no pill can cure it.

When I was growing up (we were eight children in our family), occasionally we had disagreements which I thought (at that time) were serious, and warranted to be solved by our parents. Since I was the only boy in the family for a while until my younger brother was born years later, I felt I had no voice or opinion at all because my three sisters took the center stage. Occasionally I ran to my father to complain, and surprisingly, his consistent response was "go back and work it out, you are all siblings". I did not like that sort of response from my parent; however, it forced me to face my sisters and realize that the solution to our problem was not anywhere else but in our midst. Certainly, I was not an easy kid to handle because I had a deep-seated feeling that one should not give up a fight. We argued over minor things; however, at that age they seemed to be big stuff. By now you may be wondering what then kept me in line. There were two major things which kept me in line as I remember. First, I was aware that at the end of our squabbles, in the night we will all be in the same hut, and will all eat together as a family. Secondly, we all have to reconcile before the sun set. At that age, big words such as "reconciliation" did not mean much to me. All through my childhood our parents instructed us very strongly that we should never let the sun go down with a dispute in the heart. In my case, that last part did put a fear in my heart, so much that, at times I found myself trying to remember if I had something to settle with anybody before the sun went down. I did not know and did not want to know what could happen, if I ever let the sun go down with a dispute in my heart. I imagined all of the bad things happening to me if I ever let the sun go down with a dispute in my heart. The awareness of being under one roof, subconsciously prompted us to resolve our differences. Analogously, in our global canopy as we know it, there are no escape routes. Even if you turn yourself into a fox, you will still be under this canopy (earth) and you will still have to deal with other inhabitants (wild animals/ creatures) wherever you go.

In your life journey you meet people from strange places, and people with different languages, habits, customs, beliefs, ages, gender. To complicate the situation, you meet people whose skin-color looks different. You meet young and old people, you meet rude/ inconsiderate people and also people who are friendly and genuinely helpful. In the end you ask yourself what do you have in common with all these people. By the end of the day, you realize you share "humanity" with all those people you encounter on your life journey. We all landed on this planet as babies, and for some known or unknown reasons, we will disembark permanently. The question is, what is the legacy you leave for the next generation? Let me just make very clear, the urge and need to help somebody in need of help, is not a property of any culture or religion. We are all born with it; humans are social, and there is a need to reach out for help or reach out to offer help to a needy person. The tricky part is, there is no way to tell the intention or the heart of the receiver of such a help. America still has good days. We should start by building a humane society, by taking baby steps towards reconciliation via taking personal responsibility. Uniting America should be our first priority. We should remember that harmonious relationship does not come out of arguments and finger pointing, but rather from sincere repentance, and admission of wrong doing.

CHAPTER TWO:
LIFE ON A MIGHTY RIVER

It was late in the evening; I sat on our deck facing the ravine, watching tall green trees moving their lush green branches from side to side as if they were in a dance hall having a great time. I fell into a trance-like awareness; I could not feel my surroundings, yet I was not asleep; the dancing of the green branches absorbed my consciousness. I felt lighter and could not tell where I was, but I was not asleep; subsequently, I entered another reality of consciousness. I was aware of the gentle wind blowing on my face, and I was laughing internally. Slowly I descended in a trance. I was still able to hear the birds singing, and could see the clouds moving in harmony. It was neither night nor daytime, my eyes were neither closed nor opened, and yet I observed a large wider and deeper river flowing with force, collecting everything in its path. This mighty river which runs through the lands, with its destination being the ocean of life, reminded me of our fragile beginnings and our imminent reunion from whence we came. Living is exciting and challenging at the same time, because it takes a person like me or you through the terrain of life-journey, which in fact dictates not only the principles of survival but also how to relate appropriately with the "unknown". The movement of such a powerful river in my brief but extraordinary experience left me with a life time experience. As mentioned elsewhere, analogously speaking: life is simultaneously sweet and bitter, nurturing and destructive. To be human could be the trickiest reality, that neither angels in heaven nor a devil in hell would prefer to be. I innocently assume that Angels do not have to make decisions because they are either in heaven or in hell eternally. Human beings are constantly faced with choices and decisions, and that is exhausting.

Life is made of coincidence of opposites. In life there is a coexistence of contradictory essences: weakness and strength, male and female, hate and love, justice and injustice, war and peace, satiety and hunger, birth and death, eternal and non-eternal. In this journey of life, one needs to recognize the possibility of reconciliation in all contraries. The river of life flows through many lands and along the way gathers all types of peoples, cultures, languages, beliefs and personalities. As human-beings we all embark on a journey in which unpredictability challenges our best predictions. Scientists do their best in peeking into the future, but they can never predict accurately (at least not yet). All of us are riders, and in our involuntary state of "being-ness," we are forced to share the ride with strangers who turn out to be our distant relatives with whom we have never interacted, relatives who are removed from our daily life encounters, relatives we wish we did not have. We may not like them; we may not want to look at their strange faces; we may not want to share oxygen with them. Our necks stiffen as a result of not wanting to see who is to our right or left. Our peripheral abilities are frozen, our breathing gets shallow, and we look like lifeless human statues. No wonder we convince ourselves as time goes by, that they are all alike, and they are thieves and rapists. They are degenerate and, if they are lucky, they are only "one-third" human. They have nothing better to give back to our world, to this mighty river we find ourselves on; they are suckers of the world's resources. To complicate the situation, we cannot get rid of them permanently because the DNA results show that they are actually our relatives. Yet we think and believe they are the embodiment of a curse. Their presence becomes the talk of the nation every day, and everywhere. Why did God create such people? (This becomes the conversation around the family table in the evenings). Some ask, what are we supposed to do with them? Does God really expect us to socialize and treat them as people? What is going to happen to our country, and our children? The answer to all of the above questions is: "**Yes! God expects you and me**

to love them as we love ourselves." Let us keep in mind: just because we do not have choices of embarkation, and we cannot undo the entry points, does not mean that we do not have an ability to choose how we behave and treat fellow riders who are under the same predicament. None of us chose to be born at a particular time and space. We all find ourselves in situations which have nothing to do with our personal likes or dislikes. For instance, there is nothing I can do to change my country of birth, or my birthday; yet there are plenty of things I can do to make my life-journey meaningful and productive. As riders of the mighty river of life, we have plenty of opportunities to see our souls in the eyes of strangers. We all came into this life involuntarily, and rest assured, we will exit at a certain point and time. The fascinating thing about life in general is the fact that, the more closely I get to know the stranger at my door steps, the more translucent my heart becomes. By this I mean, life here on earth can be meaningful, constructive and enjoyable if we come to a realization that no one single person has all the pieces of the puzzle.

If we are all riders in this mighty river of life, a journey we did not particularly chose, why do we look at our fellow passengers as rejects? Were you there when the Creator created what we have come to call planet earth? Did you create the ocean and the beach you cannot wait to visit in Spring? The rivers and springs you cannot wait to get to and fish, did you create them? When you were born, how much money did you bring with you? Do you own God, or did you create God, or it is the other way around? Does your being ahead of me, make you the sole owner of the land we call home? Is it greed, or do you really need that much to survive? This reminds me of something I heard a long time ago when I was a young boy. It is a story I heard from older people of my tribe (Maasai) as they customarily pass wisdom to younger generations via stories. This is the story: A long time ago when Africa was still ruled by tribal chiefs, and dictators, a certain land was hit by several years of drought. People struggled to survive with the very little they had, with a hope that very soon they would get some rains. After several years without sufficient rains, people began to starve, and many lost their livestock. Whatever reserve people had, dissipated, and they began to starve. The Chief, who had plenty of everything, decided to have two days a month in which he would have all his subjects attend a lavish banquet outside his Palace. He summoned his servants to go in every village to inform citizens of his intention. When the day came, people were instructed to sit in a semicircle facing the Palace. The chief's servants worked very hard to prepare food for all these people. The chief's guards controlled the crowd, and reminded them to face the Palace, so that everyone will have a chance to see the face of the Chief as he comes out to greet his subjects and praise them for their resilience. Some of the younger people in the crowd had never seen the Chief before, thus this was going to be their chance to see him. As the Chief was getting ready to come out to greet the crowd, a fight broke between those who were sitting in the front row and those behind, and between those who were already seated and those who were struggling to find room. The guards struggled to control the situation, because they did not want the Chief to see all that. Unfortunately, the fight was still going on when the Chief stood in front of his Palace, and he asked the head guard what was the reason for the fight. He was told people were fighting among themselves because those who were sitting in the front row, turned to those behind them, and demanded they should not be included because they had not been good and loyal citizens. Hearing that, the Chief raised his arm, and there was a dead silence. The Chief stood before the crowd and said: "All of you are my subjects. None of you forced me to do this. My invitation was for everyone who is my subject, and what you are about to receive is free. You did not work for it, and you did not force me to do this. I chose to invite you as my special guests. What gives one person a right to deny another person the opportunity of enjoying the feast given unconditionally? Regardless of your differences, you are my guests of honor, and you all deserve to be here. Welcome, and enjoy the meal." This story (true story) accentuates the necessity of accommodation and greater need to suffocate our instinctual greed and desire to look the other way from a needy human being. True, our governmental institutions are built on the principle of stratification, and our distribution of wealth is very much built on this simple question: Am I keeper of my brother? Regardless of our situation, status, age, gender or skin color, we should never forget that we are all guests and recipients of God's gifts. The more I see how we treat each other, the more I find myself going back to the story above. We should not deceive or sing ourselves to sleep in the midst of human sufferings.

Let us be honest: I know and you know that discrimination has not gone on vacation somewhere far away that we do not have to worry about it. The truth is, discrimination is thriving implicitly. In my opinion, it is much easier to fight explicit discrimination than implicit discrimination. Put it this way: I would rather live with a known vicious neighbor, than a hidden vicious neighbor. Not too long ago somebody said to me "we will never get rid of discrimination in this country". I responded to this individual by saying, "the eradication of discrimination here on earth does not look promising; however, the goal should be the identification and acknowledgement of this illusive destructive virus, which for the last few years has gained a hurricane speed which is so disruptive in our lives and turning us into brutes of the wild." Discrimination comes in different attractive colors which at a glance do not look so bad; however, at its core there is a poisonous seed which attacks human souls indiscriminately. Every one of us must remain vigilant because this enemy can attack anybody, anytime, and the vaccine is not available yet. My point is this: it is much easier to protect yourself from an enemy or danger you know, but it is much more difficult to protect yourself from a hidden or unknown danger. Since you know your enemy is within striking distance, I would hope that you will remain vigilant all the time. Of course, you may not feel comfortable in a group in which you know there is a particular individual who could fly off the handle for any insignificant joke; nevertheless, you may continue to participate and enjoy the party even though you are watching your words or any joke you might share with the group. The fact remains, since you know this particular individual in a group has a very thin skin, you might take extra measure to elaborate your remark simply because of this one person in a group who might get it wrong and get everybody upset. In this case you are not being deceitful, but rather being mindful that we are all different from each other. Even identical twins do differ in certain things. By this I do not mean you should push the dirt under the rug, and pretend that all is clean. By recognizing the fact that we come from different backgrounds and different beliefs, it would be wise to share your perception gently and wisely, because your knowledge or understanding of the issue in question remains personal, and most likely you would like to deliver it in a way that it will not make your friends or your listeners dismiss your thought right away. Gentle and careful sharing of opinions, tends to minimize arguments and disagreements in a lot of issues. The underlining goal is to create an atmosphere where issues are seen as pieces of a larger puzzle known as "life".

As a Psychologist I know that most of the time, behind any action or behavior there is a history. Every individual we encounter in our lives, regardless of gender, age, or social status, has a history. In other words, the individual you encounter comes from somewhere, and has been socialized by an environment probably not similar to your environment or upbringing. In early stages of life, one has no choice but to adopt and accommodate what seems logical and appropriate at the time. Put it this way, if an infant was able to answer the fundamental question, namely, "who is God?" I would not be surprised to hear the answer from that tiny baby saying: "mom". Environment has a lot to do with how we perceive and interpret our immediate surroundings. As a child grows and goes through various levels of development, perception of the surrounding also changes. The world of the child gets bigger and overwhelming as he/she grows up, and finds her/himself making decisions in the absence of the primary caregiver. It would not be an exaggeration to say that by age 3 children understand basic moral issues. For example, they understand that infliction of physical harm on other children is wrong. At that age they may not have all the necessary words to express their feelings; nevertheless, they can tell a good act from a bad act. At that age children have not learned yet how to wear a "persona" mask successfully; in other words, they are often blunt and straight to the point. As they grow up, they learn from adults how to circumvent the issue successfully. In our society, often we do not respect or reward the truth tellers; instead, we reward those who are good in circumventing the truth by referring to them as "smart". So, we contradict the younger generation. At the end, we sound utterly stupid when we dare to expect the younger generations to tell the truth, nothing but the truth.

Without exonerating an individual from his/her actions or choices in life, I have found it helpful in my profession to take a person's history and current environment into consideration before I draw a conclusion. It is very helpful to listen and understand a person within his/her own world before drawing any conclusion. Listening from a non-committal position gives one a broader view and understanding of the speaker. Unfortunately, many people (including those in the field of psychology) tend to rush into conclusions which might be off the target. Sometimes we (clinicians) forget that whoever asks for help, has been with that problem longer than a clinician/doctor/clergy can imagine. Listening with an open mind is noble. Yes, I understand, there are times when rapid reaction is needed to save lives, but we also know that not every day or in every moment an immediate reaction is needed to solve our many problems in our lives. Personally, I see a benefit in persuading a person to view the world through his/her own glasses. Symbolically, I do not give my patient or student, my personal glasses to view the world; rather, I do everything possible to help this individual find his/her personal glasses to view the world from his/her vantage point. In my professional work, I have met unbashful racists. I am not only talking about patients, or students, but also professionals or even colleagues; yet by the grace of God, I always managed to see the "Imago Dei" hidden deep under the obvious muddy face. Numerous times, I was tempted to draw a conclusion that these people were vicious and immoral. However, the more I waited and refused to draw conclusions, the more I felt sorry for them as victims of ill-informed and corroded upbringing. We are all recipients of our environments and upbringing, and we should never forget that; it takes time and effort to sort out what are our personal beliefs within what we innocently and unintentionally encoded in our brains. By this I do not mean that the racists (implicitly or explicitly) are not responsible for their behavior (because at the end of the day they are accountable); rather my point is: mothers give birth to innocent babies, and after that, the babies are at the mercy of their surroundings and upbringings.

As much as I would like to say I am a product of my upbringing, my life today has a lot to do with my personal decisions as I juggled between what my parents wanted me to be and what I wanted to be. I loved my parents, but at the same time I wanted to be "me" and not them. As a stubborn little Maasai boy, I made some poor decisions, and thank God, my parents did not withdraw their parenting skills; instead, they coached me gently and firmly.

Just before the beginning of WWII, my father told me not to judge a person by the color of the skin. When I asked him why, he responded "because he/she bleeds like anybody else." I did not know why he told me that, but I later figured that out. He fought in WWI for the Germans, and there he saw so much blood and destruction of lives, lives of people he never met before, strangers killing strangers without a just cause. He later said war makes people demonize the other side as a way to silence the nagging and persistent question, "why?". He said war is not personal, and many times soldiers in the midst of the battle do not have the luxury of choices. He told me that during and after the war he had friends both white and black. He got to know some German doctors who treated the wounded. Years after the war he kept contact with those who were not deported to Germany. He found that some moved back to Germany willingly, however a very few remained in Tanganyika and continued to run small medical dispensaries. As a little boy I used to get very sick, and since there were no towns, or roads then, my father would pick me up and walk miles through the forest, to an old German doctor he had met in WWI. That doctor treated me several times, and I believe he never charged my father. By the way, Tanganyika contin-ued to accommodate German Missionaries after the war, and my father had contact with them when he was considering becoming a Christian. As WWII was winding down, I got very sick with malaria with a touch of pneumonia; my father and I walked to a military camp where Polish prisoners of war were held, awaiting instructions from Europe. There again, my father knew a Polish doctor, who was allowed to treat me. Based on these incidents and many other encounters, I came to realize why my father was not prejudiced but rather wanted to judge people by their actions, not their skin color. The fact that he was an orphan who was raised by strangers, shaped his moral compass. He lived and died without knowing his mother's face. He was just a tiny baby when his mother and all his siblings died. At the age of four he lost his father, and he was left to depend on the mercy and goodness of strangers. Circumstances shaped his behavior and understanding of relationships.

During and after WWII, we heard a lot about Americans, probably due to their forceful involvement which of course ended the war. I had never seen an American, but African soldiers who survived the war came back home with a good impression of Americans. They believed their involvement helped save the rest of the world, particularly how they defeated the Japanese. My brother-in-law (John Ole Leteiva), who was a member of the King's African Rifle (KAR) special unit, was sent to fight the war in Burma; simultaneously, some of the men from our area were sent to fight the German army in North Africa. Many of those people did not survive, and families did not find out that their loved ones had lost their lives until the end of the war. In case you are wondering how Tanganyika got involved in a war which started in Europe, you need to understand that after Germany lost in WWI, Tanganyika became a British Protectorate; in other words, Britain took a role of a "Nanny". Homes were raided, and young men and older boys who looked strong were drafted into the British Army. Those Tanganyikan soldiers who encountered Americans had stories to tell about them. I was young then, but one thing I certainly heard was that Americans are kind people, strong, and friendly. However, I did not know anything about slavery, until later on in my early years of school. Later I developed a very strong desire to study American history, and that is when I encountered the brutal reality of "slavery" and its ugliness. The truth is, the knowledge (revelation) of slavery, put a big dent in my romantic and innocent imagination of America. However, never enough to kill my relentless search for a silver lining. Subconsciously I struggled very hard to experience and see or read about an "America" which can and must rise above the ugly history.

Years back (1967) I witnessed riots in this country, and heart-breaking destruction of properties, etc. Those years, the ugliest part of America was exposed for the entire world to see. I remember getting up one Sunday morning, rushing to catch a bus for church, and when I got there, the church was not there---it was burned down Saturday night. I later moved to Minnesota, and one time I was asked to participate in a panel discussion on "Race Relations". On my way to the meeting the radio program was interrupted with these words: " Dr. Martin Luther King, Jr. was shot dead". At that point I wondered if I was actually in America, the country I had always loved and respected during our struggle for independence. Those years as we struggled to get the British out of Tanganyika, we saw the glimpse of freedom light from America, shining all the way to Tanganyika. Our fight then was not over the skin color but actions and practices of colonialism.

Of course, discrimination, racism and prejudice are not and will never be defendable. But just because we find ourselves in the midst of this social and moral cancer which is destroying everything in its path, it does not mean we have to run away from this disease, hoping in the next few years it will be history. We cannot harness or eradicate this soul-killer disease through/ by finger pointing, or blaming. It is pointless to spend our energy on that because we know historically and practically the white Americans nested this deadly disease for hundreds of years. We cannot go back over three hundred years of slavery, but we can start looking for ways to show a sincere remorse for past wrong doings. No decent person can stand up in support of what white people did to people of color. However, the living generation could disassociate themselves from the past generations by creating reconciliation boards, which will listen to people's stories and collaboratively implement some changes in schools and businesses, and devise ways to help the disadvantaged people of color feel at home in America, since this is the only home they have known for hundreds of years. Both sides should learn to talk with each other and not to each other. In other words, it is between you and me, and not me and them. The past generations are gone and left us holding a chaotic world. If we do not get our act together and fix America, no one will do that for us. Put it this way: when the house is on fire, it does not do us any good to shout at each other, demanding to know who started the fire. It would be logical to call the Fire department, and while that is in the process, we must all try to put the fire out, otherwise we will all be homeless. We are all riders, and none of us can control this mighty river; let us not waste time squabbling over situations in which we have no control. Let us make the best of it.

I believe that exposing discrimination in our lives is essential. Commonsense dictates that if discrimination and racism are not exposed and dealt with through a relentless non-accusatory dialogue, chances of having a civil understanding between parties could certainly be lost forever, and we may accidently demolish any bridge of communication and dialogue between parties. I certainly believe that exposing discrimination in our lives, makes it possible to devise ways to harness it. The more we deny or cover discrimination with all sorts of shallow smiles and gestures, the more it gains strength and becomes more destructive. The inevitability of disagreements in a world is a given. However, let us not forget the fact that, in the same world, there are plenty of agreements. At times we forget that disagreements between parties can be a good thing. One of the many characteristics of democracy is disagreement. However, disagreement for the sake of disagreement is futile. Disagreement which is driven by sheer selfishness and greed, might end up in intimidation, manipulation, and egocentricity.

Imagine for a moment a ship in the middle of the ocean threatened by tempestuous weather; the crew members may have disagreements and legitimate complaints against the captain. However, a conjuncture of dangerous weather could force the crew to postpone their complaints against the captain, so they can focus on saving the ship. They cannot afford to waste any little bit of time they have at the moment in arguing and trading charges. They will put their personal issues aside and focus on the imminent threat to all of them, including the captain. This does not mean that if they survive the ordeal, all previous complaints are resolved. They still go back and find out the solution to their problems, but this time with a keen awareness of the intricacy of their relationship and how they managed to unite against the common danger. At the end of the day, they were just sailors who share a common interest: survival of the ship they have come to know as their home.

My point is this: sincere and practical disagreements often produce realistic and strong relationships. However, I do not subscribe to the belief that there is a strong correlation between "disagreement" and "argument". Just because a couple disagrees in certain things, does not mean argument is necessitated or imminent. By the way, arguments in most cases tend to harbor irrationality or cloud the facts. As humans we certainly learn a lot by and through disagreements, but hardly any important thing from arguments. Normally disagreements force people to look for alternatives or better ways to reach a goal. In other words, disagreements among family members are good because family members might be forced to re-evaluate certain rules or dogma, whereas arguments might lead to the break-up of a family. My sense is, Americans do have fundamental disagreements in civil liberties, health care, voting rights, education, and jobs. Despite those disagreements, Americans have enough sense not to set fire on their own house. This was evident during the Civil Rights Movement. I stepped on American soil in the sixties and I did not see how this country was going to hold on together. To my surprise it held together and never let outside foes set fire on America. However, we ask ourselves how America got into such an awful predicament? Unfortunately, this is not a contemporary issue in America; it has been here for so long. It has been transmitted from one generation to the next, and has been normalized by those who have had the upper hand in the country.

From a historical perspective, this country always had white and black people, but they were never regarded as equal. In 1782, Congress approved a national seal that included the Latin phrase *E.Pluribus Unum*, symbolizing the union of the thirteen colonies into thirteen states under one Federal government. This famous Latin phrase is printed on the back of every American penny, and simply means, "out of many, one"; or to put it differently, one can say," many" or "group" is a product of "individuals"; or we can also say, "individuals are building blocks of a group." Grammatically speaking, "many" and "one" co- exist. You cannot have a full understanding of "*unum*" in the absence of "*pluribus*". As one looks back and tries to understand the history of this land (keeping in mind that Native Americans were here before any Europeans or Africans stepped here) during those centuries when what we know now as United States of America was not yet born, it is not hard to see why it took so long before "The United States" was born and realized. One wonders what then went so wrong that individuals were recoiling and began to treat other human beings as "worthless and unnecessary". How did the color of the skin devalue a human being? Or can we certainly say the aforementioned Latin phrase which was adopted by United States Congress was a logical and politically democratic pronouncement in the history of this country? The phrase is inclusive and practical, especially in a country which is made up of many colors and shapes. In more than one way, the United States reminds me of a "quilt". The fact that to this very day the same phrase is still on the back of our official currency (penny) indicates that America is a country of many colors, shapes and sizes, and yet united as a nation. However, we should not be oblivious of the fact that, not too long after the adoption of this phrase, Congress adopted an insensitive, divisive, and brute-like legislative language which declared that slaves, meaning "African Americans," were not fully humans but rather 3/5 human. This statement was incorporated into the USA constitution as the infamous 3/5 compromise between North and South.

To refresh your mind, it might be necessary to look back to the 1607 Jamestown Plantation in Virginia and the Plymouth Plantation in Massachusetts in 1620. The difference between these two plantations, and the ideologies which came out of these two historical centers, divided the American soul forever. Jamestown Plantation in Virginia (established 1607) was a slave- based agrarian economy that produced a Southern aristocracy, whereas Plymouth Plantation featured enterprising capitalism, and town-centered participatory democracies. These regional interests and beliefs buried the African Americans (then known as slaves) in the rubble until the gradual birth of the Civil Rights Movement. There is a saying in several African languages which translates: "When two elephants engage in a fight, grass suffers most". Anyway, the decisions regarding the African Americans were made in their absence. The deals were reached and implemented without their input. The reason was simple. Put it this way: when did a farmer discuss or consult with a flock of his turkeys before taking them to the slaughter house? Please keep in mind (as far as European Americans were concerned) that African Americans did not reach a level of humanity until the late sixties. So in order to understand the aforementioned famous Latin phrase printed on the back of our penny (*E. Pluribus Unum*) one could arguably say, this phrase was uttered with the exclusion of African Americans; otherwise why was it that in the same period of the adaptation of this phrase, the infamous language of "a slave is three-fifths" was incorporated into the U.S. Constitution? If you take time to look at the U.S.A Constitution, Article 1 section 2, you will get the point. So African Americans who were brought to this land as slaves were not considered as human beings; also, the native people who were here before anybody in Europe knew how to build a boat let alone a ship, were not considered to be Natives but brutes. You can therefore see that the problem of racism/prejudice and discrimination had been brewing for centuries to a point where it became the "new normal". Even though early European Americans depended on African slaves to farm the land, build roads, build cities and so many other things including fighting wars, they never took the "yoke of slavery" off their necks. The more useful they were, the more they were suppressed and intimidated. They were treated like cattle or chicken; they had no rights or say in regard to their wishes. You may not get the real feel of it now, but just imagine if your parents or relatives were found in that predicament. How quickly we forget that life is a journey; once you embark on this big ride, you cannot stop the mighty river. We intoxicate ourselves with what we believe we rightly earned, and treat those under and beside us as brutes; we become oblivious of the movement of the mighty river of life. We brush away our temporary residency, and claim permanent residency in the midst of mourning of our loved ones, or those who built cities and roads we enjoy today. We lie to ourselves so much and act as if we have control of tomorrow.

You cannot change yesterday: your best chance is today and now, for tomorrow is still a wish, it is a "hope". You do not wait for someone else to change your behavior, for you are the sole person to change you. Your one positive action of respecting another human being is the best contribution in life's journey. There is an old Native American phrase which says: "before you judge me, wear my moccasins for six months, and then judge me." Have you ever been "black" before? Or have you ever been "white" before? If your answer is no, to any of my questions, then I would advise you to paddle your canoe very carefully. You are not an expert of someone's toothache, because the tooth is not in your mouth at the moment. Therefore, do not dismiss the complaints of the patient, or your fellow American as a chronic whiner. The truth is, I did not know the impact of discrimination or understand its destructive power until I was denied a part-time job of unloading frozen boxes of chicken in a certain city despite the fact that I passed the company's required test. The job manager was blunt and clear when he told me "Hiring you would mean losing all my workers. Sorry I cannot hire a black man as it stands." I felt hurt and disappointed, but not as bad as when I was refused a cup of coffee in a restaurant in the middle of a very cold winter. Unfortunately, religious institutions were not exempt, either, in the early sixties, in regard to racism. Yes, we have made progress, but we still have a long way to go in regard to equality in many sectors of our society. Please keep in mind this single and simple truth: that "equality" and "opportunity" are twins. You cannot have equality without opportunity. It is unrealistic to blame millions of poor people for their poverty, without giving them means and opportunity to pull themselves up. In other words, it is inhumane to blame millions of low-income people in this world or treat them as lazy scavengers, while at the same time those up on the ladder of stratification continue to rest their boots on the necks of the low-income people. Politicians spend valuable time creating laws which assure that the working poor will continue to be on the bottom of the ladder until they meet their death. Is it greed or just simple meanness of those born with silver spoons in their mouths to constantly blame the poor for their poverty? It seems to me most of us who claim to be religious have forgotten the fact that "poor Lazarus" is still under the evening tables of our homes, feeling hungry and neglected (see Luke 16: 19-31).

CHAPTER THREE:
SEEKING UNITY
WITHIN DIVERSITY

On January 20, 1961, on a very cold day in Washington D.C, a 43-year-old President John F. Kennedy spoke to the nation and to the world, saying: "We dare not forget today that we are the heirs of the first revolution. Let the word go forth from this time and place, to friends and foe alike, that the torch has been passed to a new generation of Americans . . . born in this century, tempered by war, disciplined by a hard and bitter peace, proud of ancient heritage . . . and unwilling to witness or permit the slow undoing of those human rights to which this nation has always been committed, and to which we are committed today at home and around the world. Let every nation know, whether it wishes us well or ill, that we shall pay any price, bear any burden, meet any hardship, support any friend, oppose any foe to assure the survival and success of liberty . . . In the long history of the world, only a few generations have been granted the role of defending freedom in its hour of maximum danger. I do not shrink from this responsibility . . . I welcome it. I do not believe that any of us would exchange places with any other people or any other generation. The energy, the faith, the devotion which we bring to this endeavor will light our country and all who serve it, and the glow from the fire can truly light the world. So my fellow Americans: Ask not what your country can do for you . . . ask what you can do for your country." (Time magazine, 1963).

Thousands of miles away from America, a group of us who were active in politics gathered around our short wave radios and listened to President J.F. Kennedy's speech as if he was a few feet away from us in Tanganyika. We were looking for any words of encouragement in our struggle to free our country from the British. Without ever meeting President Kennedy in person, I felt like he could be my brother or a person who could understand our political objectives. His words encouraged us to stay on course, and fortunately in the same year (on December 9, 1961,) under the wise leadership of Mr. Julius K. Nyerere, Tanganyika gained her independence without a shot being fired. President J.F. Kennedy was loved by many Tanzanians even though they never met him.

President J.F. Kennedy's address to the nation that Friday (1/20/1961) sent shocks of optimism around the world to all freedom lovers, and simultaneously hideous fear to the hearts and minds of dictators in all corners of the earth. As a result of such speech, Americans rose to their feet, and showered their hearts and minds with a sweet scent of hope and optimism. The speech was just what the Americans needed to hear from the young President after so many months of the campaign. However, the speech as I read it did not give a full picture of what awaited him in the Oval Office. He did not have time to waste; he inherited very difficult problems here at home and abroad. He was the first President to face the possibility of nuclear war. The Soviet Union under Nikita Khrushchev was threatening world peace. Cuba, under Fidel Castro, who at that time was the extension arm of the USSR, was proving to be a headache. American troops stationed in Europe were not uniformly welcomed, even though they were there to keep NATO intact. For instance, President de Gaulle's announcement that he would not take directions or even protection from the United States, certainly frustrated President Kennedy. The situation in southeast Asia was deteriorating. And here at home, he stumbled into the oldest and biggest problem in the history of America which his predecessors had conspicuously circumvented for centuries. Coming face to face with such an old malignant "tumor" known as "racism" was the last thing he needed on his plate. He could not ignore or walk away from it even if he wanted. Centuries of discrimination, prejudice, and racism had reached a boiling point. Industries and labor unions were having problems. Everywhere he turned, he heard and saw problems. Global conflicts were multiplying and threatening the fragile alliance established after WWII. To capture the scope of what he was facing, imagine an individual who is faced with a necessity of fighting two violent fires, one is in the house and the other one is burning the trees and dry grass near the house. How would you fight those fires successfully?

I am assuming President Kennedy was aware of the situation both here as well as overseas when he took office. Yet as a good soldier, he was going to move forward and execute the duties of his office as a President. If he worried how he was going to fulfil his obligations here at home and overseas, certainly his speech did not show any hesitation at all. He knew how to deal with world leaders, including those who suppressed their citizens. I personally know that his speech was just what we (in Tanganyika) needed in our struggle to gain independence from the British.

The magnitude of Black Americans demanding their God-given rights, probably was not on the top of his agenda. Of course, there are some lines in his speech which show that, at a certain point, he was going to address the issue of 'human rights' which he believed this nation had always committed to deal with and never made any progress. He had the best advisors in his administration; however, one could argue convincingly that he did not have the best advisors in regard to race relations. We need to realize that Black Americans were not just fighting for civil rights, but more than anything else, they were fighting for "basic human rights". They were tired of being categorized as "sub-humans", and they were no longer willing to hear the century-old term, "wait" (of course they had waited for hundreds of years and they were still treated like brutes). They were making their demands public and were letting the whole world see what conditions they had been subjected to. Under the leadership of Dr. M.L. King Jr., Black Americans consolidated their demands, which forced the Kennedy administration to respond. There were clashes between Black and White Americans, which the whole world was watching, in the early part of President Kennedy's administration. The worst was in Montgomery, Alabama, where at least 20 protesters were beaten with clubs and fists. Around the Greyhound bus station, it took about two hours before the white mob (approximately 1,000 people) was broken up with tear gas by state and city police. That incident prompted the Federal government to intervene. Government intervention caused most of the southern states to distance themselves from the Kennedy Administration. Race relations generated a lot of discussion around the country, and the old wounds of slave ownership came alive. The hidden hate and mistrust between communities came alive. America was burning, and no one had a solution to the problem. The FBI kept a close watch on African American leaders and branded them as "communist agitators."

Looking at President Kennedy's speech, it is my belief that, prior to his inaugural speech, he was briefed and informed of problems not only overseas, but also potential problems here at home. If that was not the case, what was he basing his speech on? As a pragmatic person, he meant what he said that day. As a commander in chief, he evaluated the situation and decided to meet the problem head on. Somehow, he had an idea of how his administration was going to respond to the USSR aggression, but was not sure how he was going to deal with conflicts between Blacks and Whites. In that regard his speech was firmly grounded on personal courage uttered in a prophetic language. His commitment not to shrink from his responsibility, was his fundamental belief that life can only expand in proportion to one's courage. His administration was faced with two wars, and could not afford to lose either of them. He needed to fight the global fire (communism,) but he was also aware that unless he brings the local fire under control, his efforts to spread democratic values around the world, would have amounted to nothing. I assume he was very familiar with the old saying, which says, "physician heal thyself". Looking beyond the American shores, he saw a tumultuous world. New governments were being born, and colonialism was being challenged in every part of the world. He wanted to nurture and influence these new and young governments. He wanted to steer them away from communism, yet he knew well that, unless he keeps his own house in order first, his sermon was going to land on deaf ears. In his speech, he indicated his intention to challenge the erosion of human rights not only in far lands but painfully in his backyard. Consciously or otherwise, he was including the marginalized Americans (Black Americans) in his message not to give up hope, for help is near. Unfortunately, as I mentioned elsewhere, Black Americans were very much familiar with the word, "wait," for your freedom is near. They had waited for hundreds of years, so they wondered how much longer? However, some Black Americans sensed a slight difference in President Kennedy's approach to domestic problems which was not evident in his predecessors who, by the way, stood by while Blacks and other minorities were demonized and left to live on a periphery of humanity. Thankfully, under the leadership of Dr. Martin Luther King Jr., a line of communication was established. Attorney General Robert Kennedy became the administration's lead person in this endeavor. This approach gave the President some credibility in the world, that he was a man of action and not afraid to confront those who stood on the road to freedom. He shared Dr. Martin Luther King Jr.'s vision of a United States where skin color, gender, and religion will cease being liabilities. President Kennedy (in this case with Dr. Martin Luther King, Jr.) saw a nation which would not only struggle to liberate those beyond its shores, but equally those who had been marginalized and underserved for many years in the very heart of America.

The emergence of Dr. Martin Luther King Jr.'s articulate and relentless leadership saved The United States from destroying itself. Those of us outside of the United States who studied and followed American politics for years, saw a country which was inching towards civil war. Many younger democratic governments in Africa watched the events in America very carefully. For the first time, many Africans saw the dark side of America, and began to wonder whether America's talk of equal rights was not just a talk. The details of what the southern states of America were doing to Black Americans, gave young African leaders impetus to generalize white people as hypocrites. Many turned away from Christianity, which was known then as a white man's religion. However, a good number of my generation wanted to give the American government the benefit of the doubt. We were not ready yet to turn east or anywhere else for that matter. China was not a major political power those years, and the USSR, other than quietly supporting some countries in central Africa, did not have much influence in East African countries, because Tanganyika, Kenya, and Uganda were still struggling to gain independence. It seemed like the whole world was going to explode momentarily. Just imagine, the British were being forced out of their colonies, and the French government was doing anything possible to keep her colonies intact in Africa. Therefore, to see America erupting into street fights and bombing of places of worships, was a setback. The loss of lives and property as a result of Black Americans taking to the streets was painful and regretful. However, I do not remember any real revolution which took place in human history without loss of lives. Black Americans had had enough of status-quo. They wanted to live like human beings, and not just exist aimlessly. They were prepared to face the oppressive system and demand their rights. In that struggle, people lost their lives. The oppressive system was not willing to loosen the grip, and as a result, things got very ugly. Sympathetic whites were hesitant, and wanted to take a step back to strategize as one way to avoid loss of innocent lives. However, Dr. Martin Luther King, Jr. was not persuaded to step back, so he continued with his non-violent strategy which exposed the brutality of law-enforcement and biases of the justice system.

These two great men of our time (President Kennedy and Dr. Martin Luther King, Jr.), who were raised in two very different worlds (the world of plenty, and the world of poverty), for unexplained reasons each believed the time was approaching when Americans would only be Americans. This hopeful thought was being complicated by the reality in the streets all over the country. White Americans in general believed America was changing for the better even though the change was slow and difficult. On the other hand, Black Americans felt the old "trick" was in full swing. They felt to be told "wait" was the term used for centuries which amounted to "never". Both President Kennedy and Dr. Martin Luther King Jr.'s Civil Rights Movement knew that America's greatness in the world would be measured by American greatness at home. Segregation policies, racism, and prejudices at home contradicted the image President Kennedy wanted the world to see. In other words, America's prestige as a powerful democratic nation in the world was dissolving, not from without, but from within. Corroded morals and twisted justice proved to be the greatest enemy of America. This is to say, in most cases, the worst enemy is not necessarily out there somewhere, but it is with you, or worse yet, it is within you. President Kennedy (I assume) realized that a person cannot sell a product convincingly unless he/she believes the product is good. Democracy is a good commodity, but it is hard to sell to others if the seller dissociates from it.

Both President Kennedy, and in this case Dr Martin Luther King, Jr., realized that a divided nation cannot survive very long. In some ways those two powerful leaders, during the struggle, envisioned the birth of a united America, where skin color, gender, and religion will cease being liabilities; whether that was doable or not, they shared that dream. President Kennedy envisioned a nation which would not only struggle to liberate those beyond its shores, but equally those who had been marginalized and underserved for centuries in the very heart of America. He envisioned an America which will not surrender to personal greed and selfishness. He saw a need to free not only the oppressed but also the oppressor. Both President Kennedy and Dr. Martin Luther King, Jr. recognized a need to open a line of communication between Black Americans and white Americans. At a certain point both sides (of leadership) realized a bridge must be built in spite of the hardship ahead. A bridge where two leaders walked toward each other with a hope of shaking hands, a first step of reconciliation; a sign of acknowledging the injustice and the wrongs which had separated and poisoned this nation for over three hundred years. In a corner of my mind, I wonder whether these two great men's dreams and visions were not just hope. Can we really reach a time in our human history where people will no longer see colors? Is color-blind an achievable goal? What did Dr Martin Luther King, Jr. mean in his speech "I have a Dream" when he said, "I have a dream my four little children will one day live in a nation where they will not be judged by the color of their skin but by the content of their character"? (Martin Luther King, Jr. I Have a Dream. Edited by J.M. Washington, 1992) We all keep the color of our skins, and probably the first thing people notice right away is our appearance which includes skin color. I am inclined to say, Dr. King was not referring to a state of "color blind" but rather a time and place where one is not going to be judged or evaluated based on the appearance, but by character and ability. Human character goes deeper than the skin; in other words, the real character or the real person has no color. Judging a person by skin color, is not only shortsighted, but also insane and simplistic. Cognitive misers have a tendency to look for short-cuts in regard to judging other people, and as a result they stereotype others, which obviously leads to prejudice and discrimination.

As Americans we should not let the awareness of skin color cloud the value of the person. The problems come when the "value of the subject" is embodied in the color. It is misleading to think that a human value rests on the appearance. In our field of education, we very much know that, the value of the book is not imbedded in the cover of the book. What really counts and is meaningful is the content of the book, or in case of a person, what counts is the character, or what a person has to offer. Both these two leaders knew the waiting games were over, and there was an urgency of establishing a line of communication. Black Americans were not out to destroy America, they were in the streets to revolutionize America, for America was and still is their home.

African Americans were tired of being told to wait for their freedom. They were tired of being treated like animals, robbed of their dignity. For hundreds of years, they had heard the sermon of tolerance, they had heard promises from those who continued to rob them of their human dignity. For hundreds of years, they heard promises from politicians. They were told justice was on its way, meaning a day of liberation was so close. Religion was used to hypnotize them and put them in a trance-like situation. For centuries they patiently waited for that day on which they will achieve "humanity". Their oppressors made sure that they remained in the dark. The law of the land was written by the European Americans for the European Americans, and it disregarded African Americans and Native Americans. For hundreds of years African Americans were used in building this country, including cities, roads, and farming--- all that without a chance to share the fruit of their labor. In spite of religion being used by the oppressor as a tranquilizer to keep the slaves submissive, it never killed the deep-seated thirst for freedom. The voices of the "oppressed" people got louder and more intense. The whole world was watching slavery in action, and the agonizing screaming of the oppressed people caught the world's attention. Those images of American streets made people wonder whether there is a heaven; and if there is heaven, to which heaven did the departed African Americans go? Is God white, too? Who created people of color? If people of color are worthless, why did God create them?

Christian churches used the Bible (Colossians 3:18-23) to justify slavery and suppression of women. If you happen to be a person of faith and believe that there is a God who created us all and the entire universe, help me understand the concept of "slave and slave-master" which seems to linger in the history of mankind for centuries. Please pause and visualize "Slaves and Slave-master" before God Almighty who created the visible and the invisible, a Creator who is the ground of life, a Creator who is beyond and above finitude and infinity. Between "slave and slave-master," which of them can claim to be free? The "slave-master" or the "slave"? From an anthropomorphic perspective, I cannot imagine God smiling at these two groups. My childhood and simple religious understanding of God's purpose does not include one person telling the other "you are not any better than a bull or a cow in an auction." It does not include the incremental theology, one which suggests that slaves must treat their masters with the greatest respect or count their masters worthy of all honors. I have a hard time visualizing the face of my Creator and Savior watching millions being stripped of their dignity and birth rights and being auctioned and owned like materials.

Slavery comes out of a sinful nature, just like death itself. Therefore, slavery cannot be justified religiously or politically. It robs the human soul; it clouds the Imago Dei in a human being. For those who spend countless days attempting to sugar coat the ugliness of slavery, and apply "incremental movement approach" as if slavery was a logical progression needed to reach "ultimate ethic," these people are not doing religion a favor at all. Slavery was and shall remain "evil". Yes, there are so many things we cannot explain in the world; sometimes our attempts to theologize or explain certain events tend to make things worse. Slavery is evil, so should we say God was asleep when heartless and brutal slave-masters were abusing the defenseless? I believe God saw the evilness of slavery before it happened, but just as God did not stop Adam from making a wrong choice, that does not mean that slavery was God's choice. We need to remember that God created a person with a free will, one who is free to believe or not to believe. The foreknowledge of God does not necessitate the event. The actor remains responsible, not God. Those who enslaved others cannot claim that God made them do it. They made their choices based on their greed and paranoia. The slave master is also a slave of his/her own desire to oppress. Yes, the slave master is not free because he is constantly finding ways to maintain dominance. I would say the oppressor remains anxious and constantly worried that the "oppressed" might get free and subsequently exact revenge. The oppressed also has a problem: he/she remains angry, and suspicious of any move by the oppressor. It is not unusual for the oppressor or the oppressing group to show some sincere attempts to reconcile with the oppressed group, but these attempts may be rejected by the oppressed group right away, saying, Why now? What changed? After all these years of abusing and suppressing our group, why would you be sweet all of a sudden? How do we know that you are sincere this time? Therefore, a deep distrust between the oppressor and the oppressed remains.

Both groups, before the throne of God Almighty, are desperately in need of mercy. Both sides consume much energy holding their positions, and cannot see beyond themselves. Therefore, both sides need to be redeemed from their self-destructive positions. Slavery did not only happen hundreds of years ago; the reality is, slavery is alive and well. The tactics and approaches have changed, but it smells like slavery, walks like slavery, and hurts like slavery. Yes, you hardly see people in chains, but the chains of today are worse because most of the time they are mental and emotional chains. Our repentance should not just be for what the ancestors did, but for the slavery we practice in our schools, churches, businesses, politics, and in the world we live in. The paranoia of the unfamiliar faces, languages, customs, habits, and beliefs, drives many of us to adopt an ethnocentrism concept. Many times we lock ourselves in our own little safe boxes for the fear of losing control of what we believe to be ours and only ours. We create bubbles around ourselves, for the fear of being contaminated by those who are not like us. We get in a habit of learning religion, but we fail to live it. We are slaves of our own egos, and may Almighty God redeem us and remove the mental chains, and open our hearts to reach out and not to recoil when we are faced by unfamiliar circumstances.

So, you may ask me a fundamental question after all I have said so far, and that is: is there any hope for our nation, or are we ever going to live and treat each other as human beings first and Americans second? In spite of all the disagreements and discontentment I mentioned above, there is hope that a new nation shall come out of this old and rugged nation which has been intoxicated by years of greed and self-centeredness. America is not beyond redemption. America still has the gentle caring soul despite a bit of a messy face.

CHAPTER FOUR:
GRANDMOTHER'S QUILT

I grew up in a country and a culture in which grandmothers played the role of "family-consultants," which amounted to advising the younger mothers pertaining to health of the babies, etc. I had never heard the term "quilt" until I came to America, even though I had seen similar material as I was growing up. However, these patches consisted of old and soft hide, and were sown together by older ladies or grandmothers whose daughters or daughters-in law were expecting to have babies. The pieces of hide to be used were softened by a perpetual motion rubbing until these little pieces of hide became so soft and without wrinkles or roughness. After rubbing with some sort of oil, the hide is folded and stored until the arrival of the new baby. A grandmother or a mother in-law puts a lot of value into the making of this little but deco-rated hide to surprise the new mother. However, I had never thought much of it, because Maasai boys or young men were never encouraged to ask their mothers or grandmothers the significance of that material. However, I saw new mothers in the village holding babies wrapped with that soft hide. Keep in mind, Maasai never depended on clothes found in towns. Put it this way: our domestic animals were not only the source of food, but also a source of what we wore those days. Whatever we slaughter for food, becomes also a source of clothing for ourselves. Thus cattle, goats and sheep were useful in several ways. Donkeys were only useful for transportation. Nomadic life dictates how much one wants to keep dragging from one kraal to another, especially when the rains become unpredictable. During the moving from one side of the land to another, the donkeys carry most of the essentials on their backs. As mentioned, I had never heard the word "quilt" until I came to America. And my memory or knowledge of what other tribes did in regard to preparation of a new arrival would not necessarily be correct. It is estimated that Tanzania has more than a hundred tribes; therefore, it would be misleading, let alone an unnecessary burden, to dip my feet into a field of social anthropology at this time.

When I first saw a quilt (here in America) I did not make a connection at all. However, one of my colleagues at a clinic, had one in her office hanging on the wall. Because it had many colorful patches stitched together, I casually asked her why she had that sort of blanket hanging on her wall. That was the day I heard not only the word "quilt," but also why patches and different colors and shapes maintain their uniqueness and connected-ness simultaneously. I was impressed by the meaning and symbolism of that quilt. One day in my office, after seeing clients all day, as I sat to dictate my notes, the idea of a quilt came to me. I realized I could use it as a counseling tool. The next morning, I walked to my colleague's office and asked her to tell me where to get a quilt. I told her I had discovered how to use a quilt as a counseling tool, and also a teaching tool when I had group therapy sessions. It has been the most valuable tool I ever used in clinical work and in teaching psychology for over forty years. I gained a deeper perspective of a quilt. I learned that grandmothers made quilts for their grandchildren. The design and creativity which goes into making a quilt, has very little to do with affordability; rather it has everything to do with memories and the bond between the grandmother and the new grand-baby. This means grandmother's quilt is absolutely special because it preserves a lot of memories of a new parent to be and a hope of a new baby to be born. It is where the old gracefully join hands with the new dawn. It is where the continuity of yesterday merges with today, and it is where "then" and "nowness" consummate to assure a "tomorrow". Normally the patches which will end up being stitched together do not have the same color, and some of them are larger, some are older, and sometimes the material and the texture could be different. It is assumed that each patch has a special memory and meaning to both grandmother and the mother to be.

The quilt was made from a mixture of material. Grandma very skillfully selected the patches, but very intentionally. Some of these pieces are big and some are small, some have unique shapes, while others are low key. Some are red, some are blue, some are green, some are black, some are yellow, some brown, and some have no color, but are white instead. How did Grandma do this? All these pieces did lay separate at first, until Grandma picked those pieces which were impregnated with historical meanings. Days and nights were spent piecing the masterpiece together to create a beautiful work of art, and memories to last forever.

Like Grandma's family quilt, our world is rich in diversity. A quilt is made of many parts. . . patches, cloths and string all woven together to form one concrete reality. If parts of the quilt are missing, it would be incomplete, and could be used as a rag to clean up the milk on the floor. However, as a united quilt, it is warm and comfortable. It could be used to curl up in on a chilly night, or to lay on, on a warm summer day. God lovingly created each of us to be part of His quilt, and it would be incomplete if one square were to be cut out. Size does not dictate the importance; the arrangement may seem strange at times, and colors of patches may clash, yet that is all part of the beauty of the quilt. The squares on the quilt can each represent a moment in one's family or a member of the family who departed. The squares can also represent religious significance such as baptism, confirmation, or bar-mitzvah, etc. As I look back more than seventy-five summers ago, I can still see my great-grandmother's facial expression as she assured me that I will get over the malaria. I can clearly hear my great-grandmother singing to me and wiping tears off my chubby cheeks with a soft leather cloth. I know she promised then to be with me and help me in times of trouble. Yes, she was taken away from me, but I will always remain grateful for the little cloth she used to wipe my tears.

Just as my great-grandmother taught me not to discriminate against people or blame them for things they could have avoided, I discover (as an adult) her words to be a great help in regard to getting along with people, even those who discriminated against me. When I was abroad, away from my home, I was able to remember my great-grandmother's advice. I met all kinds of people: gentle, cruel, rich, poor, healthy, sick, and people with different skin-color. She taught me to trust God even when things seem hopeless. As I experienced life in Europe, I was able to believe that God has put all of us here for a purpose. The whole world is God's quilt. He placed some of us around the mountains and some in the plains. Just as grandmother's quilt is always intentional, so is God's quilt. He has chosen us with great care to be His work of art; our existence and our "being-ness" are not accidental; we are both parts of the quilt and recipients of God's grace.

Sharing dwindling resources is one of the most difficult challenges of our time. I remember being worried as a little boy because my mother had a habit of inviting strangers whenever my father slaughtered a goat or a bull. However, she would always assure me that I would not go without, and added "food would not taste good without guests." When I was not quite happy with my mother's rationale, I went to my father with the same concern; he responded, "there is a good reason for a person to have two arms: one arm is for receiving and the other one for giving it away. You do not have to be a friend of a receiver; as long as the person has a need, you cheerfully give, for in so doing you may be entertaining the messenger of God unknowingly." These early lessons did shape my behavior and my outlook of life in general. Watching the changes in the world and the struggle between the "haves" and the "have nots," and the real possibility of conventional or nuclear war over the world's resources, I wonder whether we ever learn anything from history. Why did God create a quilt of nations and cultures? Why do some live in tropical areas and some in places like Norway? Or to put it differently: are some of the patches in God's quilt more important than others? As a patch on God's quilt, what authority does any person have to dictate to the little patch next to him/her? If God did put that patch there, it seems prudent to seek God's will before passing judgment.

The frustration of differences is not unusual in life; however, that does not mean acting upon it impulsively is going to bring much-needed relief. I believe Jesus Christ had something to say about judgement for those who profess to be Christians:

> Do not judge, so that you may not be judged. For with the judgment you make you will be judged, and the measure you give will be the measure you get. Why do you see the speck in your neighbor's eye, but do not notice the log in your own eye? Or how can you say to your neighbor, 'Let me take the speck out of your eye,' while the log is in your own eye? You hypocrite, first take the log out of your own eye, and then you will see clearly to take the speck out of your neighbor's eye. (New Revised Standard Version, Holy Bible, XL Edition. *Matthew 7:1-5.* 1989, pp. 888-889).

There is even a harsher requirement for Christians to think about before we destroy those who do not act like us or believe like us or think like us:

> You have heard that it was said, 'You shall love your neighbor and hate your enemy.' But I say to you, Love your enemies and pray for those who persecute you, so that you may be children of your Father in heaven; for he makes his sun rise on the evil and on the good, and sends rain on the righteous and on the unrighteous. For if you love those who love you, what reward do you have? Do not even the tax collectors do the same? And if you greet only your brothers and sisters, what more are you doing than others? Do not even the Gentiles do the same? Be perfect, therefore, as your

heavenly Father is perfect. (New Revised Standard Version,
Holy Bible, XL Edition. *Matthew 5:43-48.* 1989, p.887).

My great-grandmother never knew how to read or write; however, she
celebrated differences (diversity); she did not appreciate assimilation, but
rather respected acculturation. She did not want the big patches to swal-
low the smaller; she believed the world is better when each person is given a
chance to grow and adjust. Well, today we have a lot of opportunities, and
technology has broadened our horizon so much. We have more possibilities
beyond our parents' dreams. Today's accessibility was not even yesterday's
dream. We are too focused, however, on what others have, and very little time
on what we have at hand. We tend to look outward instead of challenging
ourselves. I do believe creativity begins within. To put it differently: staring
at your neighbor's beautiful lawn, does not automatically change your lawn
into a well-taken-care-of place. You need to use all the tools at your disposal
to improve the situation.

To share my visual imagery, I would ask you to close your eyes for a
few minutes. Now imagine you are standing somewhere else and you can
observe the world we live in as a huge quilt. Imaginatively, you can fly over
it, under, and around it. With such extraordinary ability, you are able to see
all at a glance. The big ball known as planet "earth" is solidly fused and deco-
ratively covered with colorful patches connected by one mysterious thread.
Some patches look rugged, and some look very new. Some colors are much
brighter than others, some patches are much smaller than others, and they
are all in different but unique shapes. In your world of imagination, you
discovered something unusual, and that is, these patches can actually talk,
and share their feelings. Now, after all the imaginative experience you have
had about this quilt, and the knowledge you gained during your observation,
how would you react when you encounter a patch which is trashing other
patches just because they are shaped differently, or because their colors are
not attractive or they are located or placed on some far away corner of the

quilt? If you were to speak the language of the quilt, what would you tell the "bully-patch" which insists on the extraction of certain patches because they do not meet his/her standard of living?

To articulate my point, let us suppose you have a beautiful quilt for sale, and let me assume you want $500 for it. You put an ad in a local paper, and as a result, a couple who are expecting a baby in a few weeks show up at your door steps. This couple wants to buy the quilt that they saw advertised (they liked the colors of the quilt as it appeared in the newspaper). I guess you would be very happy to get a buyer in such short period of time. However, before they pay you, they decide to inspect the quilt. In doing so, they discover that two or three patches are missing. Your immediate explanation to them went like this: "I extracted those patches because they were shaped funny, and their colors were not attractive." I suspect this couple would not pay you the $500, simply because the quilt is no longer "whole." The extraction of one patch violates and deviates from the "wholeness" of the original quilt. The maker and designer of the quilt stitched those patches together with a particular purpose in mind.

I am convinced we can all learn several things from the quilt analogy, namely: (a) every patch has a significant meaning and purpose to the quilt-maker; (b) every size, color, shape and position of each patch is intentional and important; (c) all patches, regardless of color, size, shape, position, or texture are related and connected by a single thread; and (d) all patches rest on one solid piece of cloth. So, as you stand there staring at the colorful patches of all sizes and shapes, you realize what you are looking at are not two quilts but one quilt. This is to say: in "many" there is "one," which is an undeniable truth. The world we live in is very colorful. It has all kinds of patches, and there are no two patches which look exactly alike; yet we need to affirm our stand in the world and see that our energy should not be spent in futile attempts to extract others from God's given quilt; rather we should celebrate the differences and make attempts to look for the "positive" first before we condemn.

My dear brothers and sisters, stop and think for a moment. The reality is staring at us: we are all new comers, immigrants and strangers; no one was here when God created what we have come to know as our world. Truthfully, *every* person you meet or encounter, even bullies at your work-place, or people at the super-markets, religious functions, or on the road home after a long hard-working day, has a function which you and I may never fully understand in our short residency here on earth. It is much easier to blame the product at hand, and never bother to question the intent of the designer. Do not forget that you are just a "patch" on God's quilt, and every patch's existence matters regardless of color, gender, age or socioeconomic status.

Today we live in a diversified world, and the convergence of all these cultures and languages should not be viewed as accidental revelation. The truth is, diversity is as old as humanity itself. The earth we call home has been immutably diverse in its natural design. Just because mankind is becoming aware of global diversity, does not mean that global diversification is a new reality. I cannot think of one thing which is detached or stands outside of the undeniable presence of diversity. The more one pays attention to weather changes globally, the more one catches a glimpse of diversification. The rich information we gain through men and women of meteorological centers around the world, certainly solidifies my previous claim, that the world was designed with "diversification" in mind. The weather changes, the landscape and many other differences, such as peoples, languages, habits, customs, foods, and beliefs--- all these confirm my belief that, in some strange ways, you and I are related. You are my brother and truly my sister. The issue is no longer the authenticity of global diversity, but rather why we spend so much time nullifying the obvious? We go out of our way to look for things which divide us, rather than things which unite us. There is so much more to be gained from diversity and acculturation than from sameness. Thank God, we can never be the same. The thought of sameness is not only illogical but unattainable.

A human being was created with a concept of subjectivity and objectivity. The core of a human being is permanently encapsulated in the brain with the internal desire to relate outside of "self." In other words, a normal person is born with "I-Thou" capability. I believe God created us to be accountable and responsible for our own actions, and at the same time we cannot have a meaningful "me" without "you." "I" and "Thou" are inseparable realities in this life. A desire to reach out, is natural, and no one should feel shameful about it; in the same breath we need to accept and realize that someone's need to reach out to you for help or comfort is natural. What I have been trying to elaborate is the fact that life is a two-way road. Putting it differently: subjectivity and objectivity affirm each other. They give each other meaning; in other words, you cannot understand the importance of one without the other, despite their differences. Subject and object are interdependent. Simply put, the world would be a very confusing place if we all talk, eat, walk, act, think, and look the same. If you cannot tell a difference between you and everyone else in your community, I assume you might end up in a psychiatrist's office. I therefore postulate that, when all cultures are permitted to contribute and share their perspectives and goals, the world (canopy) which we call "home" benefits immensely. Each and every culture is unique, and it is my sincere belief that every culture, regardless of its origin, is special and valuable. Truthfully, there are no inferior cultures; all cultures are super cultures. By this I mean those people with different habits, languages, beliefs, looks, are not from inferior cultures at all; rather, it is personal ignorance of these cultures which makes one think of these cultures as inferior in comparison. We should not forget that our judgement of others is subjectively based. At this point of my life, I am inclined to say: that which is fundamentally different from the ordinary, should be taken as a challenge rather than a threat. We all need to remember that any threat, being real or imagined, potentially generates fear, defensiveness, and eventually panic. Most of the time, decisions made based on panic, tend to deviate from reality and logic. By the way, I am not attempting to dismiss the reality of "fear" at all. We all know that "fear" is also useful in our lives. What I am rather pointing out is the dual function of fear. Despite what we think of "fear," it is a tool woven into our mental system which raises a red flag when an unfamiliar situation or stimulus gets closer to the perimeter of our "ego safe zone." This is to say, fear is a necessary part of life, which should not be eradicated but rather managed properly. Of course, "fear" saves lives. For instance, fear prevents us from walking into an oncoming car, or jumping into a lake without any swimming experience. We should not fear "fear" itself, instead we should be wary of elusive fear, which paralyzes our cognitive abilities.

As human beings, sometimes we seem to have a desire to erect safety zones, and it terrifies us if a stranger invades our space. In most cases we do this, not because we are full of hate of new people on our block, but because we are afraid of losing control. As I understand it, "loss of control" remains the most feared reality in humanity. The desire and the appetite to control not only ourselves but also our environment, tends to germinate discrimination and racism.

Let me elaborate the term "discrimination," since its usage is critical at this juncture. The term discrimination as it stands remains controversial because of the feelings attached to it and the intent of the user. In 1954, Gordon Allport, a pioneer in the study of personality traits, wrote a book which was the earliest comprehensive discussion of "prejudice". He based his remarks on a significant body of scientific research. According to him, discrimination usually has meant directing more negative behaviors towards a particular group, compared to others, but may include having more negative thoughts and feelings about some groups relative to others. In other words, people can be discriminatory in regard to their feelings and thinking, just as they are in terms of their behaviors. It should be noted that, in most cases discrimination is usually preceded by "prejudice," which, by the way, is a felt or expressed antipathy based on a faulty and inflexible generalization, and may be directed toward a group as a whole, or toward an individual because this person happened to be a member of this particular targeted group. (Allport, 1954). Scientifically and linguistically, "discrimination" does not always have a negative connotation; it is useful, for example, in making choices. Noting a difference between two friends may help you select an appropriate birthday card for each; or noting a difference between two cars in a show-room might be helpful in case you were looking to buy a car. Most of our choices we make daily, for some strange reasons, involve discrimination to one degree or another. To differentiate usually implies the conscious or unconscious enumeration of many differences, whereas "distinguishing" frequently means to note the different identity of an object.

In my opinion the term "discrimination" cannot be understood in a vacuum, meaning that without the awareness of the "object" being a person, thing or thought, the "subjectivity of discrimination" remains irrelevant and mute. Analogously a bullet in a chamber of your firearm was designed to inflict pain or kill the potential enemy. However, this same bullet can stay in a chamber of your firearm as long as you want, without ever inflicting pain or killing anybody. This does not mean the destructive nature of the bullet has disappeared just because it has been dormant for a long time. Likewise, "discrimination" is a bullet in a chamber of a human nature. The term "love" which is not objectively revealed, does not necessarily lose its positive nature; however, it can remain dormant and fruitless. Loving yourself is a given; it is something expected of any normal person; however, the challenge is objectivism. Many Christians are familiar with these words: "love your neighbor as yourself". My personal understanding of this requirement is: any love which is genuine must not be barren. In its membranous center lies the anthropomorphic image of God (Imago Dei). The central seed of love or rather the built-in desire to reach out to the "other", that instinct of giving rather than receiving, or that urge to serve rather than being served; that type of flame in the human heart can never be ignored or suppressed by mankind without a major consequence.

It is my fundamental belief that mankind is not created for him/herself, but rather for reaching out. Just as a bullet is filled with explosive materials, similarly a "love" which is alive is designed to emit reflective layers of divergence. The frozen, locked-up "love" in a human heart remains worthless and self-destructive. Love can only make sense when it has its object. Whereas discrimination seeks to demonize and dehumanize the "object" for fear of domination, "love" establishes a line of communication which eventually leads to "trust" between the subject and the object. Whereas hate and paranoia erect fences and high walls all around, love establishes communication and builds bridges between "peoples". Notwithstanding the unfamiliarity of the new faces, these strangers in our neighborhoods (and the other side of our national borders) do actually have basic human needs just like everyone else in this world.

It is absolutely appalling to read or hear how some leaders of industrialized countries can separate children, including infants, from their mothers for months in the name or rather under the pretense of border control policy. We label and treat those at our borders (who are in search of decent working conditions) as hard-core criminals. We do not want to see and treat them as individuals, but rather as a group of criminals. We do not see them as individuals who are seriously looking for ways to feed their families. We sentence them without a "trial". They are guilty regardless. If one of them has committed a crime, then all of them are criminals. We do not want to treat them as individuals, but rather as a group. They are all the same, and we treat them as we treat a national virus outbreak. These so-called thieves and potential criminals and rapists are tried and condemned before and without a court hearing. The message being preached by the rich and industrialized nations is clear and simple: "these new faces at our borders are infested with crime, and they are not any better than the brutes in the wild". I am sorry to say, only the feeble-minded people believe that "evil" has a color or gender. If you think of it, how many people of color were involved in some of the brutal wars which went on in ancient European countries? I have been in many countries in Europe and Russia, and all these countries have prison buildings. For some unexplained reasons, these prisons are occupied not by people of color or refugees from poor countries, but actually by natives of the industrialized countries. Many years ago, before I went to England, I had a strange belief that there were no thieves in England; I was later puzzled when I actually saw prisons in England. My point is: crime does not discriminate, despite the effort to sugar-coat some crimes as "white-color" crimes. A crime is a crime. For instance, a person who knowingly refuses to pay tax as required by law, while everyone else pays taxes as required by law and without delay, that person could and should be classified as a "national thief". Unfortunately, as humans we tend to give ourselves credit by projecting evil to someone else, for in that way we can live with ourselves. The reality is, that sense of contentment is false and does not last very long.

Distancing ourselves from millions of human beings who are desperate and in need of a simple glass of cold water, or a piece of bread or just a tent to call home, those whose homes and villages have been destroyed by evil regimes; turning them away by branding them as thieves and rapists, or locking them in uncomfortable and restrictive places, cannot be anything else but modern day "genocide". Those who claim to be religious while condoning such inhumane policies, need to know that such actions put them in the same room with Cain in the Old Testament, who responded to God saying: "Am I keeper of my brother?". You may be devoting your time reading the Bible or Koran, or any other religious scriptures, yet one thing you need to know, is this: faith without action is a dead faith. Do not use your religious holy book as a cover; get up and stand to be counted. Those people you treat like garbage are real people with essential needs like you.

Industrialized countries need to go back to the root of the problems and help these nations get on their feet. To throw them back to where they came from is like sending a neighbor of yours back into a burning building until the fire fighters get there. My point is, these strangers at your door steps are "every man and every woman" you meet daily in this life. The greatest strength of America, apart from military superiority, is her diversity. In diversification there is a "give" and "take" mentality. There is character building, and sharing of talents which individuals possess uniquely. A nation or family can be diversified without being divisive. We need to demythologize the popular old myth of the melting pot and replace it with something practical, realistic, and workable. The truth is: we are all patches on the "quilt" of life, and the quilt is not complete or beautiful when some patches are removed.

CHAPTER FIVE:

THE SLAVE TRADE AND THE TRANSFORMATION OF AFRICAN CULTURES IN NORTH AMERICA

Before we get any farther in our conversation, I would like to explain and clarify the issue of this term "minority" in regard to people of color. We need to understand that when we speak of "minority" we are not only speaking about those with black, brown or tan skin, or those who seem to have fewer numbers, but rather we are speaking of all those with less voice and less power in the system. A good example is South Africa, where the majority black population had been under the white, racist government until a few years ago when former President Nelson Mandela took over the leadership of the country from an oppressive and racist "apartheid" system. Skin color itself does not have magical powers; it is the meaning attached to it which makes a difference. The term "majority" has very little to do with numbers. Globally, there are more people of color than white people. If that is the case, how did the minority (white people) dominate and set up rules and laws that gave them an upper hand for centuries? Without going into so much explanation, I would like to entertain three major areas of human life, namely: culture, religion (spirituality) and language. Those three blocks rest on the palm of "geography" which shaped and reshaped, and nurtured human behavior and language.

Since I am now discussing about people of color in America, I would like to begin by commenting on the transformation of African cultures. For many years now, historians have argued inconclusively whether "African slaves" were able to maintain African cultures and influence in the new world. Of course, these slaves had cultures, languages, religions, before they got to what we know now as South and North America. They brought their entire "beingness"; however, the nature of the slave trade itself, and the reality of life as a slave in this country, made it impossible for African cultures to survive unchanged in America. Many different cultures were represented in the slaves who arrived in this country. This was very different from European settlers, who often came to America with large groups of people from the same country or even town or family. These more homogenous groups usually settled as a group in the same cities, towns and regions in the new land. The slaves brought from Africa, however, did not come as a homogenous group. The slave boats often purchased slaves at two, three, or even more ports in Africa, and the slaves may or may not have shared a common language or some cultural practices with others on the boat. Furthermore, when they were brought to auction, they would often be mixed with slaves from other regions. The slave buyers had no particular interest in keeping countrymen (and women) or relatives together, and sometimes purposely chose slaves from different regions to lessen the possibility of the slaves organizing a revolt. Despite these barriers, some slaves could eventually find other slaves who spoke the same language, came from the same general area, and shared some cultural traits. In general, however, slaves could not transfer one language or one common set of customs, rituals, and beliefs to life in this new land.

I hope you understand that at this point of our lives we are not in a position to explain every step of the horrible period the African slaves went through; yet I feel we have an obligation to pause and take a look at what happened to those people who found themselves being sold and bought like cattle in an open market. The evil and immoral African chiefs who sold their fellow Africans, as ways to silence opposition or as a way to enrich themselves by receiving personal gifts from foreigners, were just as evil as the ones who bought these slaves. Put it this way: they European buyer, and the Americans who consciously went out to buy another human being as if buying a piece of farm equipment, are not any better than the first seller in Africa. The seller and buyer have no room or place in humanity. Keep in mind, African Americans did not choose to be here; they were brought here and stripped and denied their right to be 'human beings." The collaboration between the slave seller and the slave buyer shows how soul-less mankind can be. Just imagine how you would react if somebody treated you as a worthless creature for just a year. African Americans for hundreds of years had been treated as "door-mats." If doormats were to speak, they would probably ask to get a break. If you deprive someone a culture, language and religion, at the end what is left of the person is "nothing;" that person might as well be a rock. There is no greater death than the deprivation of religion, culture, and language.

As varied as were the cultures which the slaves had known in Africa, the slaves did manage to create a new common culture with other slaves, a culture that drew on similarities or at least discourse in religious and ideological beliefs, music, art, dance, cooking, clothing, and ways of working the land (for those who came from agricultural areas). Of course, they had to adapt to a different climate, and that impacted clothing choices among other things. And they were always at the mercy of the masters, who decided what food they were given to prepare, what and how much cloth they were given to clothe themselves, whether they were allowed to marry, and whether they were given permission or time to sing, dance, or congregate with other slaves. This new, common culture was also heavily influenced by the dominant European American culture. Some of the slaves had encountered Europeans in Africa, along trade routes or in trading centers. But in Africa these Europeans were guests of the Africans, whereas in America they were the dominant and ruling group. By being forced to live and work in the dominant culture, the slaves naturally adopted some of the European American culture.

One very important element of culture that did not survive well in the slave world, was language, even though, as Thornton (1998, p. 212) points out, language is the most stable of cultural elements. Because of the diversity of the geographic origin of the slaves who were brought to America, a slave may not have encountered anyone else who spoke his or her language on a plantation or in a domestic household. Even slaves who married may not have shared the same language. When people of diverse languages are living and working together, a lingua franca is likely to develop (Thornton, 1998, p.212). A lingua franca is a language used as a common language between people whose native languages are different from each other. The slaves in America needed to communicate with each other and their masters, so they developed a third language, similar to their masters' language in vocabulary, but with a grammatical structure similar to their native languages. Often the children of African-born slaves grew up knowing this lingua franca (Creole language) as their native tongue, thus decreasing the chances that the native language(s) of their parents would be preserved in the American world. But there was some degree of language preservation, especially in songs (Thornton, 1998, p. 217).

One aspect of African culture that survived better than others in America was the aspect of aesthetics (Thornton, 1998, p. 221). This included art of all kinds (painting, sculpture, colors and design on pottery and cloth, styles of clothing, to name a few), as well as song, dance, and ways of cooking. Aesthetics was the aspect of African culture that was more easily shared and appreciated between slaves from varying regions in Africa, and was even appreciated and sometimes adopted by European Americans. I keep certain items of African art and clothing in my office as a way of keeping me grounded and connected to the land of my ancestors. We owe a debt of gratitude to those slaves who, in spite of long hours, terrible working conditions, and dehumanizing masters, managed to find the time, energy, and resources to sing and dance and create works of art. They have given following generations of African Americans a sense of their African roots.

CHAPTER SIX:
THE CIVIL RIGHTS MOVEMENT: ARE WE THERE YET?

Centuries of dehumanizing treatment of slaves, which continued to be experienced by African Americans even after the "emancipation", sowed the seeds of what would come to be known as the Civil Rights Movement. African Americans were never pampered or favored by the relatives of their former slave-masters. They labored and suffered with a hope of achieving the status of "humanity", they cried and agonized, they shed blood for the only country they called "home", they prayed and sang with hope that Almighty God will remove the shackles of oppression from their necks and ankles. The more they prayed, the more the executioner squeezed the oxygen line. For three hundred years they struggled to earn the status of "personhood", and had been told to wait, for their freedom was on the way. Some thought and hoped that after all these years of waiting for European Americans to acknowledge African Americans' contribution in nation building, the European Americans who controlled the system should have enough sense to correct the many wrong things which had been done to African Americans for many years. They (African Americans) eventually realized no one was going to hand them their God-given dignity and freedom peacefully. They decided to join hands and go after their rights, and they did that with a full knowledge that no colonial power ever granted a colony freedom without a fight. Like any revolution, there were always those groups which hesitate to engage the "oppressor". And there were those who were convinced that the only sure way to gain their independence was by force. Fortunately, Rev Dr. Martin Luther King, Jr. devised a less violent way, which would lead African Americans out of social/mental/physical oppression non-violently. That was a wise thought, however not everyone wanted to grant the oppressor more time of trickling-down equality. The oppressor's time had expired over a hundred years ago. Most of the younger generation of African Americans concluded that the oppressive regime would never remove slavery chains off the ankles of African Americans without a fight. That being the case, they decided to take to the streets, and show the whole world the dark side of America. They were willing to shed their blood for the freedom they had been waiting for, a freedom which kept moving away every year. They wanted to know (without any more delay) whether European Americans were going to honor the constitution or not. These groups of African Americans were not oblivious of the ruthlessness and brutality of the law enforcement, especially in the Southern states, yet they wanted their freedom so bad and were willing to die for it. Dr Martin Luther King, Jr. had the same goal, which was to force the white government to free the African Americans and remove the yoke of slavery off their tired sore necks. The only difference here was, Dr. King wanted freedom without violence; he was convinced the white government had to make some major changes, such as moving from an "exclusive" to an "inclusive" approach. The timing could not be better. His determination to confront the oppressive system coincided with the installation of a new and dynamic President J.F. Kennedy. The oppressed and neglected Americans had a measurable hope in this young man, who did not just talk like ordinary politicians and evasive bureaucrats, but rather as a soldier, and a man of action. In his speech to the nation, he raised the bar to a level which gave the oppressed Americans a small window of the future, a vision of a new garden where the seed of freedom will germinate and grow, slowly but surely.

Consciously or otherwise, President J.F. Kennedy in his speech to the nation was also including the marginalized Americans and the neglected millions globally in his message that they should never give up hope.

America was going to lift the freedom light higher to expose the oppressor. Unfortunately, African Americans heard the phrase, "wait, for your freedom is near". Even though African Americans wanted to give the new President a chance to implement his policies, they worried that a single, fair-minded democratic President, may not be able to turn the tables single- handedly. They had waited for centuries; how can they expect him to change a racist system to a more democratic and fair system? Notwithstanding the President's friendly gesture, African Americans declared their intention to free themselves from the suppressive system using all means available to them.

Analogously speaking, a government stands and functions as a "parent" where its citizens are not only nurtured, but also protected by the government. Thirty-four Presidents, by nature of their obligations, saw and heard the screaming of African Americans for centuries but did not intervene; they played deaf, and blind. They were more concerned with their own prestige, and political ideologies. What kind of a parent will tolerate bullying and abuse in the family? Is it not just common sense that anyone who witnesses a criminal act and does not intervene or report to the authorities, is no better than the perpetrator? Years of discrimination and prejudice in America sank in the American psyche and became normal. After generations of discriminating and treating African Americans as imbeciles, it began to feel like treating them contrary to that would be unjust and abnormal.

Generations of White Americans who were brought up and parented by racist and segregationist parents, grew up believing that African Americans are the lowest creatures on earth. There is no hard proof that people are born racist, however all people have a potential and sometimes the ability to become racists. This by no means an exoneration of younger generations, but rather an attempt to show how this disease managed to go so long without intervention. From whence do children receive their first life instructions? Who are the most significant people in a child's world? Without demonizing parents, one needs to ask: who are the first and most primary care takers of children? Parents are the primary guiders of children at least in the first few years of life. However, children make their own choices as they grow up (I do not subscribe to the concept of "tabula rasa".) They reach an age where they cannot continue to mimic their parents, and the choices they make then, are based on their own interpretation of their surroundings.

Why did it take blood shed for a government system to listen to the very people it promised to protect and govern? Where I come from, "blood" has both a mystical and spiritual significance. For many African tribes, blood is life itself. One who is willing to shed his/her blood to save another person, becomes not a friend for life but a true brother/sister for life. Treaties which are sealed by blood are never to be broken. Symbolically, blood represents the ultimate sacrifice mankind can offer. It also stands as a "total willingness to start fresh". By the way, it is not unusual to associate "pain" with "blood". While the shedding of blood could be interpreted as a pinnacle of two opposing forces, with it comes the expectation of a shared new beginning. The line of communication between the two camps emerges and the threat of total destruction is aborted.

With the establishment of a dialogue between Black Americans and White Americans, the survivability of America as a democratic nation began to emerge. The blood of those who died during the struggle shall forever be honored and remembered by future generations. Out of chaos came order, out of segregation came integration, out of disunity, the seed of unity was planted, and there was a sigh of relief in the world. The struggle and perseverance of African Americans was evident in President Kennedy's speech. He reminded all Americans that they were (then) the heirs of that first revolution. As I mentioned elsewhere, I cannot remember any revolution in history which did not shed blood. I am not insinuating that President Kennedy was saying blood shed was imminent; however, he was being realistic by preparing Americans for oncoming necessary shocks. He wanted the new generation to stand firm and to boldly cross that line of yesterday, and step in the new fresh morning, and charge forward into the uncharted horizon. He motivated Americans; however, he did not want them to think that a proud and strong

America was going to come without a price. In that speech, Americans were being urged to open their eyes and look at the world and their own country in a new way. For America to be a leader in the world, it had to change her attitude and behavior about her own citizens. It was obvious in the minds of many Americans of that era, that Blacks and Whites were forced to confront the old malignant tumor known as "racism". Yet White Americans were not willing to give an inch; similarly, Black Americans were determined not to retreat an inch; as a result, the country was heading into a horrible collision. However, as mentioned elsewhere, under the leadership of Dr. Martin Luther King, Jr. a line of communication was established between the Kennedy administration and the oppressed Americans. There was a deliberate struggle and attempt to build a bridge between the new and young administration with African Americans who were tired waiting for their "humanity" to arrive and be recognized. Today as we look back, we realize that ordinary citizens, young and old, and leaders of that era, paid the ultimate price just to free both the oppressed and the oppressor. Today Blacks are still black, and the Whites are still white, yet they have one thing in common: humanity. America will always remain a multiracial/multicultural nation which is rich with traditions. Diversity does not mean divisiveness, and certainly variety should not lead to discrimination, but rather to the concept of complementarity.

Once in a while I hear some people raising concerns, which actually turn into personal fear, that this country is heading to "communism," and by that they mean the country is forcing people to be the same, and taking away people's uniqueness. I admit that is a concern which is a far-fetched conclusion; however, there is great a difference between "sameness" and "one-ness". As a nation the goal is not to establish a concept or philosophy of "same-ness" (which for some people sounds attractive and harmless), but rather to work towards "one-ness". The road to "sameness" is a road to stagnation and a death of a nation, in other words a blunt suffocation of a nation's consciousness. Any relationship built on sameness, besides being boring and simplistic, stagnates the relationship. The lack of "otherness" in regard to "being-ness" is a highway to the abyssal absence of "I-Thou" relationship. For a relationship to last and remain productive, both sides must contribute and complement each other. The beauty of a nation is built on the ability to diversify its talents. When I think of America or any nation, the picture I get in my mind is that of a human body. Without going into details, a normal person functions better when all of his/her body parts function in concert or rather, harmoniously. I am one person, but I happen to have various components of what is known as a "body" which I know as "me". In other words, out of "many" comes "one". As a human being, every part of me is important and its function is essential for survival. If for strange reasons my left leg goes on strike and refuses to fulfill its duties, it will cause disruption, and I might not be able to function as I would have under normal circumstances. Similarly, the function of the eyes is essential and necessary; however, that does not mean the eyes are more superior than the legs, etc. The function of all parts of the body are important and have to function collaboratively.

Similarly, a nation is made up of many parts, and each part is expected to function according to the assigned duties. If these parts cannot function harmoniously, definitely the nation will self-destruct. A fear of variety tends to generate distrust, anxiety, and stagnation of creativity. Yes, Americans took to the streets during the Civil Rights movement; people got killed by cowardly brutes, there was brutal exchange of verbal abuses, and finger-pointing went on relentlessly. At the end of all the anger, America survived, and proved to the world that it can get back on its feet and continue to face the future with hope, a hope of an America which President Kennedy and Dr. Martin Luther King, Jr. prophesized in the sixties. No group or segment of the American people is more important than the rest; no culture, religion, gender, skin color, social economic status, country of origin, or profession, should be given special treatment or viewed as less important. Anyone who loves and wishes America well, and is willing to shed blood for this country, should be regarded as an asset and not a liability. America is a multicultural country, and that is an advantage that it has in our globalized societies.

One semester during a class discussion, a student asked me if I think or believe that we are where both President Kennedy and Dr. Martin Luther King, Jr. hoped America to be. In other words, the student's question in brief was: "are we there yet?". Without hesitation, my answer to the question was: "Not at all". During other class discussions the students pointed to the election of President Obama as the strongest evidence that America has changed. I did agree with the students, that Barak Obama taking the oath of Office of the Presidency that January 20, 2009, was a 21st century miracle. It felt like a miracle for some of us who had witnessed American cities burning during the Civil Right struggle, and lived with fear of being picked up any time by Police for walking suspiciously or driving through a white neighborhood; or for some of us who saw buildings burned to the ground by unknown groups; or for some of us who were never expected to get an "A" grade for a research paper while the friends whose papers I helped to write, got "A"s; or for some of us who could not walk into a Walgreen's store without being followed by somebody aisle by aisle, to make sure that I did not put anything in my pocket; or for some of us who by walking into a restaurant made customers drop their jaws and stare more than necessary. Yes racism, and discrimination, was an "all out" war, and nobody seemed to know the solution. For me to see a Black American walking into the White House, not as a visitor but as a resident, was emotional. Many of us could not believe our eyes and ears, that after three hundred years of being viewed and treated as sub-human, finally Black Americans earned back what was stolen from them; they earned back their God-given dignity, their "humanity". Yes, I cried, and thanked God for giving me an opportunity to witness the miracle which the world will never forget. Friends and foes alike were shocked. His success to be a party's nominee presumably angered those who wore out their knee-pads praying for his failure and misfortunes. These home-grown enemies of democratic values, made sure that he was not going to receive the courtesy granted to his predecessors, despite the fact that he won his second term without a scandal. He treated, and saw people as Americans first before party affiliation came into play. He respected differences (political), but he held his head higher than the usual partisan argument; he was true to his oath of office that is to be and remain a President of all Americans. I am sorry to say the hard-core conservative groups in Washington pulled every trick in the book to assure that his Presidency would amount to nothing. Fortunately, God Almighty was not in their pockets, and their prayers never amounted to anything.

President Barak Obama took the oath and occupied the White House when the country's economy was literally buried in the trenches. American men and women were losing their lives in a war which was based on a failure of intelligence. It was a time when Osama bin Laden was laughing and drinking his tea/coffee in Pakistan and was organizing his barbaric attack on Americans. President Obama's predecessor promised to bring Bin Laden "dead or alive", but unfortunately, his term ended and he walked out of the White House before fulfilling that promise. President Obama made many attempts to build a bridge and a line of communication between the two parties; numerous times he gave the other party the benefit of the doubt, only to find out the other side never really wanted to work with him as a President of the country. President Obama did something else extraordinary before the end of his tenure; he went after the one enemy who was difficult to capture or neutralize. After Osama bin Laden directed the attacks on America on September 11, 2001, he disappeared. It was very difficult to pinpoint his whereabouts because friendly countries remained mute in regard to his whereabouts. Even though some Muslim countries said they condemned his brutal killing of civilians, they knew his hiding places but did not want to share that information with the western governments for fear of retaliation from Bin Laden's organization. After the attack on America, our government suspected two countries: Pakistan and Afghanistan. The Obama administration worked perpetually to stop this monster who instructed feeble-minded people to kill innocent people. Certainly, the Administration's careful plan did work. Bin laden was killed in his hiding place, a building in Pakistan. This individual proved to be difficult to track down and the most difficult enemy to capture; however, American ingenuity and steady military leadership sent a clear warning to present and future foes not to tempt American patience, for America will always defend Americans and friends in the face of aggression. The Pakistani government's claim that it was shocked by the fact that Bin Laden was nesting in Pakistan, is not believable. President Obama's decision to neutralize such a monster who killed so many people indiscriminately, was justified and commendable. In spite of all the aforementioned observations, I told my class that it was going to take more than one miracle to get America where Dr. King and President Kennedy were hoping. This is to say, mission is not accomplished.

The disputes between Police and Black Americans are rubbing salt on wounds and widening a gap between Black Americans and those who are supposed to protect them. Black Americans in many communities see themselves being treated as guilty until they are proven innocent. I was born and raised in a culture (Maasai) where crime has no color, gender, or even age. It was in 1967 that I learned that crime has a color. I was new to American life and got more than I bargained for. However, I can sincerely say America has changed and made notable progress, even though it has a long way to go yet before we can convincingly say both Dr. King and President Kennedy's vision of America is at hand. Of course, the election of a Black American to lead the nation in the 21st century can never be ignored by historians, and his Presidency accentuated the differences in how to build a united America where the pursuit of freedom, equality and compassion stands as a focal point. He was the right man for the job. His hard-working demeanor, and smart decisions, pulled the country out of recession. He also managed to pull the country out of Iraq without weakening American military might. He dared to look at the poor and sick in this country and engaged the nation in the discussion of how to take care of our sick people. He did not have a perfect plan (never claimed to have one), but he continued to tweak the Affordable Care Act, with a hope that those who had been marginalized (in regard to health care) could also be brought into the fold, since the essence of the duty of a President is not only to serve the rich, the educated, the healthy, but also the poor and the sick. His Presidency jolted the American history; in spite of its historic significance, however, there is still more work to be done. There are many voices and interests in America. At times competing ideologies give an impression that America is going to burst in flames, or that some states might break away and form their own countries or states. The beauty of America is the fact that, groups shout at each other, and individuals get louder and nasty, yet at the end of the day, they all know in their hearts that they are Americans, and they can face an external enemy as a united country. So, when one experiences disunity, one should keep in mind that there is a strong, and real, invisible unity within the obvious disunity.

Certainly, there are a lot of disagreements in the world; but let us not forget that in the same world there are plenty of agreements as well. At times we forget that disagreements between parties can be a good thing. Keep in mind that, among many characteristics of democracy, disagreement is one of them. However, as mentioned elsewhere, disagreement which is driven by sheer selfishness and greed might end up in intimidation, manipulation and egocentricity. My point is: sincere and practical disagreements often produce realistic and strong relationships. I do not, however, subscribe to the belief that there is a strong correlation between "disagreement" and "argument" (as previously mentioned). Just because you disagree with someone in your life, does not mean "argument" is imminent. As mentioned elsewhere, we learn a lot via our disagreements, but hardly any important thing from arguments.

CHAPTER SEVEN:
WHO IS MY NEIGHBOR?

You probably know your neighbor very well, to a point where you sometimes discuss issues pertaining to families, etc. In other words, you feel very comfortable exchanging ideas once in a while. The level of trust and comfort is there, and you find it offensive to be asked this question (Who is my neighbor?), after all you do for your neighbor. By this I do not mean your neighbor is a trusted friend you can confide in. As you already know, each and every one of us is very special, for no two of us are exactly the same. Each with a different name, and different story. She may live in Nairobi, Kenya, while he lives in Denver; her skin may be white, and his skin may be tan. Somehow, we are all related, and are bound from the time of birth. This world is a meeting place; we all enter through birth and leave via death. We may look different, yet we have that in common. How do we determine one individual is a neighbor, whereas the other person is not a neighbor? What constitutes neighborliness? Or put this way: what does it take to be a neighbor? I believe each person has some specific things to look for or expect from a person to be a neighbor. This means the answer is in the eyes of the beholder. By this I mean, what constitutes a neighbor for me may differ from someone else. My great-grandmother had an idea that a neighbor is someone or anyone you encounter in life who might need your help, or someone to whom you may turn someday for help.

To underscore my point, let me share a short story my father told me years back, before I knew how to read or write. (Those days school was a luxury and a privilege for the elite, particularly Bantu tribes who happened to have ties with Colonialists). Maasai learned their history through stories which the elders told, mostly during the evenings when all the cattle were well-secured in the kraals. You may wonder why I bring up this story, and what it has to do with the topic in question (neighbor). The story has to do with a self- contented and righteous person who could mistake his own sibling for a thief or a killer. A tendency to stereotype and devaluate the other person could result in tragedy. My father said: "Many years ago in Maasailand, there lived a man with his family in a settlement which was not too far from a place known as a 'Embusel'. The man was moderately rich; he had a lot of cattle. His two sons took care of the cattle on a daily basis. One evening after all the cattle were back in the 'kraal' for the night, the oldest son went to his father, and informed him that he was leaving home in search of a new life style. His father was shocked and saddened. The mother pleaded with her son, and the father asked him not to leave, but the young man would not change his decision. His younger brother was saddened very much, but he could not change his brother's mind."

"In spite of his parents' disapproval, the young man left and disappeared that evening. The area was well known to have not only lions, but other dangerous animals. Months and years went by, and nobody heard anything about him. Finally, the family gave up any hope of seeing him again. One evening, the second son went to his father, and informed him that since the moon was shining, he would like to visit another settlement not too far away from their settlement. Apparently, he had visited the settlement before, and in his first visit to that settlement he had met a beautiful girl; now he was eager to learn about her parents. He promised to be back very early in the morning to take care of the cattle. The father had no objection; however, he reminded him to be careful, and that he should be armed appropriately because he might encounter lions or other dangerous situations. The young man took off with his parents' blessings. He had his spear, and wore his sword. He walked cautiously and defensively. Halfway through the trip, he saw an object walking towards him, and he immediately assumed the worst.

As a warrior, he decided to meet the danger head on (customarily a Maasai warrior never runs away from a fight). He began to raise his spear and walked slowly toward the oncoming object. Initially he thought that it might be an animal, and the more he got closer, he realized the presumed animal was also moving slowly toward him. Because the moon was shining, he eventually realized that it was not an animal but a person who was also armed. Just as a few yards separated them, he ordered the stranger to identify himself immediately. The stranger did so by invoking the name of his clan. The young man also responded by invoking his clan. With just a few feet separating them the young man asked, "what is your full name?" When the stranger responded, they both startled, and realized they were not just from the same clan, but they were brothers. At that point they lowered their spears and hugged. They walked back to the settlement that night, and the parents were ecstatic, not only because the lost son was back but because bloodshed was averted. Your neighbor might be your distant relative; remember, you share the Creator who is our parent above all."

In this story we learn a few things, namely: (a) be quick in observation but always cautious and slow to react. This means what I see and hear is just half of the story. The truth is I cannot always free myself from my "subjectivity"; and (b) it is much easier to destroy (kill) the less familiar than a friend or relative. The closer you get to the other person, the more you discover yourself in the eyes of this person, and it gets very difficult to destroy this person. The further you push a person from you, and demonize that person, the easier it gets to kill that person. In this story, had the younger brother thrown his spear at the time he was assuming that an animal was coming toward him, he would have killed his own brother. Instead, patience from both sides reunited them. We human beings share the earth; we are under this huge canopy, and we all want to survive. We are all in need of something, and most of the time the resources are not equally distributed. Therefore, our canopy is colorful and uneven.

Of course, the Darwinians might have something to say about the world's stratification and inequality. Most of us are very much familiar with the unfriendly relationship between Socialism and Capitalism, which continues to trade charges. These two blocks forget that, or rather deny the reality that we (so far) share "earth" until someone comes out and says there is another life-sustaining planet in our solar system. Until then, you and I need to learn how to live together, or rather enjoy the journey of this life until our souls are absorbed into the sea of eternity. The canopy we live in has all the essentials, but we need to learn how to share them adequately. There are certain things which demand rapid reaction (for instance, evacuating people from a burning building, accidents, and so forth); however, most decisions in our lives do not call for impulsive actions as some might think. The idea of not responding immediately to a perceived danger (real or imagined) goes against human instinct. By nature, human beings are self-centered, and the core tendency of the human soul is to draw and suck in all that is perceived to be less threatening to the "existence" itself. In doing so, we hold others as suspect, and potential enemies of our own existence. Due to irrational fear, we forget that these very people who do not look like us, or speak like us, are our fellow riders (neighbors) who are also being swept down-stream by force of the mighty river of life. Every passenger (rider) shall surely end up leaving everything familiar behind and be absorbed into the eternal ocean of existence. Everyone you meet in this life is your neighbor and relative.

In summary, as human beings we should know by now that whatever is in our present shall pass without our inputs. The towers we build, the machines we build, and our own good looks, shall pass, and there is nothing we can do about it. We build and adore our successes; at the same time, we know our obsession with all these will be in the hands of the next generations. Time and time again we fail to differentiate or notice the difference between "ownership" and "stewardship." We forget that our role in the world is to remain faithful "stewards" of what we found in this world. We have to admit that, often it is when we view ourselves as owners of this planet (earth), that we begin to stratify the system. It is when we struggle to get to the top of the ladder at any cost that we do anything to demonize the other person/neighbor. In feudalism and caste systems, the rich rest on the top of the ladder, while the poor wait for the crumbs to fall off the table.

In my great-grandmother's mind, a neighbor is someone you can call when your house is on fire, a person who does not keep scores. A person who gives help freely. She told me so many stories; many of them did not make much sense then, but now I wish I could remember all of them. I treasure my childhood memories, even though it has been many seasons since my great-grandmother sang a gentle and soft Maasai tune to me. To this day her soft voice continues to resonate clearly in my head. She was over a hundred years old, she went blind, and when seated together with my grandmother, it was not easy to differentiate her from my grandmother; however, her distinct soft voice and her upright posture gave her away. She did not die; rather, after she blessed my mother and my father, they all three shared the Lord's prayer, and then she said "goodbye, peace be with you" in Maasai ("olesere"). And then she disembarked. She crossed the line and entered into "invisibility". I assume you also have similar or different memories in regard to your relatives, things you treasure in your heart and soul. Sweet memories that never get old or diminish. Do you remember the children in your neighborhood when you were growing up? Do those memories keep you sad, or do you wish you could treasure them for a long time?

When I was growing up the world was a vast place; today I live in a more compact world. Technology and a need for a better and qualitative life style is generating a "boundary-less" generation. The world has become a big village with all kinds of people who may not share goals; yet its survivability depends on interdependence. For instance, in the October 2006, issue of "Observer", Dr. Morton Ann Gernsbacher posed a question: "Who's your neighbor?" In response she wrote:

In 1988 I organized an international meeting solely by email
... These days I could not only organize but hold the entire
conference via the Internet ... In these days when computer
files of just about any kind can be exchanged with the click
of a mouse, when not only conferences, but research projects
and multi-institutional program projects can be executed
on line, when we use the Internet not only for text but also
for talk, complete with a white board, does it matter whose
office is next door to mine? ... With whom do you immediately share your incite, excite, or insight? Do you walk down
the hall to a departmental colleague's office, strategically
arranged during hiring to be near yours, or painstakingly
situated through a series of woeful space-discussing faculty
meetings which led to gnarly discussions of area groups?
Or, in less time than it would take you to walk down the
hall, journal in hand, have you emailed the PDF to your
dearest colleague, your most active collaborator, the psychological scientist with whom you are the most simpatico,
and who just happens to live in Australia? (Gernsbacher,
Morton Ann. Who's Your Neighbor? *Observer,* A publication of Association for Psychological Science). 19 (10).
2006, pp.5,22.

This line of thinking makes the whole idea of national physical borders
questionable if not irrelevant. Should there be a national debate on the definition of the term "neighbor"? What do we actually want to convey when we
speak of "neighbor"? One could assume that Dr. Gernsbacher was referring
to physical proximity in her article, yet there is a possibility she was referring
to that individual within one's professional group or social group. I am not
sure what she had in mind, yet I am inclined to say technological advance-
ment is diversifying our world much faster than many of us dare to admit.

Whether one turns to religion or social psychology in search of the definition, the term "neighbor," with all its fluid characteristics, embodies: communication/relationship; and accountability/responsibility. One can choose to have a positive or negative communication with a co-worker, or one can decide to view his/her co-worker's problem as something in which he/she feels partly responsible or accountable. In other words, one may choose not to ask: Am I keeper of my brother/ sister?

Your neighbor is possibly anybody you might come in contact with in your life. This person might be old, young, male, female, pink, black, yellow, brown, white, educated, uneducated, rich, poor, sick, healthy, homosexual, lesbian or heterosexual. The main issue here is not who is next to you or who do you meet in the street, but rather how do you treat this person. I believe most Christians are somehow aware of the words found in Matthew 25: 34-46.

> Then the King will say to those at his right hand, come you that are blessed by my Father, inherit the kingdom prepared for you from the foundation of the world; for I was hungry and you gave me food, I was thirsty and you gave me something to drink, I was a stranger and you welcomed me, I was naked and you gave me clothing, I was sick and you took care of me, I was in prison and you visited me. Then the righteous will answer Him, Lord, when was it that we saw you hungry and we gave you food, or thirsty and gave you something to drink? And when was it that we saw you a stranger and welcomed you, or naked and gave you clothing? And when was it that we saw you sick or in prison and visited you? And the king will answer them, Truly I tell you, just as you did it to one of the least of these who are members of my family, you did it to me. Then he will say to those at his left hand, You that are accursed, depart from me into

the eternal fire prepared for the devil and his angels, for I was hungry and you gave no food, I was thirsty and you gave me nothing to drink, I was a stranger and you did not welcome me, naked and you did not give me clothing, sick and in prison and you did not visit me. Then they also will answer, Lord when was it that we saw you hungry or thirsty or a stranger or naked or sick or in prison and did not take care of you? Then he will answer them, Truly I tell you, just as you did not do it to one of the least of these, you did not do it to me. And these will go away into eternal punishment, but the righteous into eternal life." (New Revised Standard Version, Holy Bible, XL Edition. *Matthew 25: 34-46*. 1989, pp. 910-911).

Those words take away lame excuses for not helping that stranger at your door step, or at the border of your country. How many times have we turned our heads away when a stranger or desperate person asked for help? How many times have we turned our heads away whenever we see a person at a street corner, begging for help? How many times have we turned away those who are struggling to earn a living? Do we turn them away because they do not look like us or they do not speak the language well? How many times have we ignored the elderly, or the mentally challenged? How many times have we used our businesses to make unreasonable profit so we can stay higher on the stratification ladder? How many times have we robbed our fellow citizens by not paying taxes like everyone else? How many times have we robbed women by not paying them fairly just because they happened to be women? How do we justify our practice of moving our companies overseas where natives of those countries make a fraction of a dollar at the end of 12 hours hard work? At times we forget that Western industrialized countries are either directly or indirectly responsible for many corrupt dictatorship regimes in the world. We share the blame because we know what these rulers are doing to their citizens, and yet turn a blind eye. We have been bad neighbors; in other words, we only show others one hand, that is a hand to receive from others; and in the process we have disabled our other hand, which is a hand of giving to others.

Of course, it is possible for one to challenge the above Biblical quotation (Matthew 25: 34-46) in light of what happened not too long ago (I mean that awful incident which took place on 9/11, destroying thousands of innocent lives) and another situation which tested the resiliency of Americans when millions of undocumented immigrants took to the streets demanding basic human rights forfeited due to their unlawful entrance to this country. The creation of Homeland Security was a very good thing, because security is in the minds of many Americans. However, one needs to understand that, "terrorist" and "immigrant" are not synonymous. One might argue, there is justification to link terrorism with immigrants because of what happened on 9/11. Such argument will not go very far because it is based on illusory correlation. Just because most of those who committed such barbaric acts were foreigners, it should not give impetus to the legitimatization of stereo-types and prejudice. My friends, evil has no color, race, gender or culture, and to pin it on a certain group of people is unrealistic. Those who end up at our door steps are not necessarily evil. They are people, they have needs, and they have feelings like everyone else. Let us face it, most people do not cross the borders to get here because living conditions in their countries of origin are wonderful. But they also do not get here to stand on a line and beg for bread. They come here as proud but desperate people wanting an opportunity to work and feed their families.

For those of us who claim to be Christians, we need to remember that our Judeo-Christian scriptures are filled with stories concerning immigration and the plight of immigrants. For instance, the spiritual father of the world's three great monotheistic religions---Abraham---stands as the archetypal immigrant (Genesis 12: 1-3). Abraham's act of faith in the one true God was manifested in his willingness to leave his homeland for a land that God would provide: a land that would be a foundation for descendants as numerous as stars of the sky. As you recall, centuries later, Abraham's children would be led out of a land of slavery into the Promised Land by Moses (Exodus 12:14). At this point I want to point out something many of us have never given a thought, that is that Africa, which has been discounted and trashed by Western civilization as the "dark continent," played a major role both in the Old Testament and the New Testament as a refuge place in time of trouble. Abraham was led to go to Egypt and survived there as an immigrant until the situation changed in his homeland. In the New Testament, we should not forget where Joseph and Mary went when Herod was frantically looking to kill baby Jesus (Matthew 2:13-15). Migration, or rather moving away from danger to safety, is not new. If ancient Egypt was able to accommodate strangers who were in trouble and needed some basic essentials, why, in the 21st Century, are we so paranoid? Yes, there could be some risks in inviting strangers into your home; the question is, when are you going to get a 100% assurance that you will certainly be safe all this year? Remember, every second in your existence is a gamble; you cannot be 100 % sure you will be alive tomorrow, so you are riding on "hope to be." Nobody expected that the perpetrators of the 9/11 attacks, who we had welcomed into our country and treated as friends, had evil intentions in their corroded psyches that would result in the killing of so many innocent people. However, we should never allow panic and generalized fear rob us of our love to help those who need our help. To dwell in a generalized fear and anxiety, would be playing into the hands of the terrorists. Unfortunately, the tragic event of 9/11 turned out to be a gold mine for opportunists whose goals were to demonize all immigrants who happened to come from the Middle East countries. At times we forget that the federal building in Oklahoma was not destroyed by a border crosser, but by a home-grown terrorist. Thus, the fear of newcomers is irrational, and it is a lame excuse not to give them an opportunity to pull themselves by their own bootstraps. There is an urgent need to clear the confusion regarding illegal immigrants; that is, if their services are acceptable and their taxes are legal, then they should also be protected by law of this country. Let it be clear, other than Native American tribes, we are all descendants of Immigrants. The argument which has been floating around for many years now, that those whose ancestors migrated first to what we now know as America, have the undisputable right of ownership of what is known as United States of America; this argument does not pass a legal test. The natives of this land were here before everybody else from European countries and Africa came here. This country was a "country" way before Columbus mistakenly set foot on this country by default. He spent several months cruising the islands of the Caribbean searching for China and Japan, and since he thought he had reached the Indies, he called the people of the region Indians. It was only in 1507 that a German cartographer who read the report of the new world by an Italian sailor (Amerigo Vespucci) decided to label the new region "America". The name stuck and was used for both North America and South America. By the way, the islands Columbus explored in the Caribbean became known as the West Indies. The point is, both North and South American countries were inhabited for many years before people learned how to build ships which were able to withstand the powerful winds of the oceans. So why does a group of "newcomers" have the right to refuse another group of desperate people to come in, not to beg for food but to earn a living?

CHAPTER EIGHT:
HUMAN RELATEDNESS

Humanity is faced with two realities and must choose very carefully. As mentioned elsewhere, mankind is designed not only with the ability to recoil but also with an ability to reach out. To put it differently, a human being is normally expected to be able to inhale and exhale. I have yet to see or meet a person who can survive for hours or days by inhaling continuously without exhaling, and vice versa. The fact that our lives depend very much on these realities, actually solidifies my basic belief that we are created with basic abilities to give and receive; the duality of life is fundamental. No one is self-sufficient, contrary to popular belief. Putting it differently, no one is safe until everyone is safe. As a young boy, I often heard my father (referring to work with the cattle or the land) saying to his friends, "you are not done until your neighbor is done". To put it in a contemporary thinking, one could say, no nation is safe until all nations are safe. Often, we are tempted to recoil and assume the fetal position in search of tranquility and safety, and we forget that the safety and survivability of the fetus depends on the mother's physical functioning.

As human-beings we are confronted with these two realities; unfortunately, we cannot just pick one and throw the other one away. Yes, they differ in their nature, however they play a big role in our lives. We depend on walls to protect us from the wind, animals (intruders) or anything else which might disturb our personal and private lives. We normally feel safer when we are surrounded by walls, and have a sense of privacy. Unfortunately, something like Covid-19 defied that logic. Despite the fact that walls are useful and practical in many ways, we should not forget that walls were never meant to be a solution to many of human problems. As a Maasai boy, born before WWII, there were no cities or building structures where we lived; therefore, I was more familiar with fences than walls. My parents were blessed with three daughters before I came along. As a Maasai boy, my natural goal and expectation was to grow up and become the best Maasai warrior. When I was about five, my father expected me to take care of the calves during the day when the rest of the cattle travelled some distance in search of green pastures. At that age I was expected to get up very early in the morning and walk into a muddy kraal to separate the calves from their mothers until the milking was done. I very well remember many mornings that I had to struggle to separate the calves from their mothers by forcing them into some circular areas surrounded by thorny-branched walls. My duty was to make sure that these calves stayed there until their mothers were led out of the larger kraal in search of green pastures. After a while I lost interest, and began to find reasons not to get out there every morning to separate calves from their mothers, which caused such unhappiness. I began to sympathize with the calves, wishing there was another way of keeping them happy. Once in a while I found myself wondering what if somebody separated me from my mother at such a young age? Even at that age I began to see the good and the bad usage of fences. I thought it was a cruel thing to separate little ones from their mothers. A few years back when my present country (United States of America) separated over 500 children from their mothers in the 21st century, I was reminded of those thorny walls which we erected to separate little calves from their mothers. It has been many years ago when I helped build those fences. Years later I began to evaluate the purpose and legitimacy of those fences. The fence kept the calves in and at the same time kept the mothers out. I sometime think if I had been able to speak "cow-language" and ask those cows how they were feeling about the fence which separated them from their babies (calves), I suspect they would have disapproved of such un-natural and cruel treatment of their babies. Yes, walls and fences are still essential in some situations; however, we need to realize that a wall does two things simultaneously, namely: shutting someone out, and at the same time shutting you in. The wall prevents the person inside from seeing the outside, just as it prevents the one outside from seeing the inside. The wall becomes the block for both sides. The wall does not only limit one's vision, but it also gives a false sense of security. A typical example as I experienced the function of the wall, was during the dry seasons in Maasai land (Korongoro, Piaya, Loliondo, In-dulen, Siringet, Engutoto, Naperera etc,) when younger boys like me traveled with warriors (ilmuran) many miles looking for green pastures for the cattle. At times we traveled several days before green pastures were located. Usually, a few warriors would be sent ahead of the cattle to locate the safer areas to erect temporary kraals closer to green pastures. Sometimes it took a few days before these warriors returned with good news that they had found a suitable area for the cattle. While some of the warriors were looking for the green pastures, the younger boys were always left with another group of warriors to tend the cattle and protect them from lions or other predators during the nights. While younger boys tended the cattle during the day under the watchful eyes of two or more warriors who were always armed, other warriors (ilmuran) worked tirelessly all day, securing an area for the cattle to sleep in the night. They usually erected high secure walls using branches of thorny-trees to protect cattle in the night. When all the cattle were in the kraal, these warriors with their spears took turns watching the cattle all night. They constantly paced back and forward with their spears and swords ready to engage any predators. This is to say, the height of the walls did not bring us total peace as one would have expected. I then realized that as long as the danger is out there, "walls" of any size or height do not guarantee "peace," which was the objective of building the wall or a fence.

I now believe that the physical or mental walls we erect to keep a perceived danger out, and embrace our imaginary peace within, could be a very tricky business. Therefore, my advice to the reader is this: before you erect a wall around yourself, or before you make a great effort to fence someone out, please understand that those walls will not guarantee you a lasting peace. You may end up pacing all night or all your life for fear of danger which might be real or imaginary. Speaking of safety, not everybody sees a necessity of building a wall for safety. Nevertheless, there are a lot of people who cannot fall asleep without having a hand gun (loaded) next to the bed, and probably other powerful guns in different parts of the house. Reports of people mistakenly killed in the night by their own relatives are alarming. A few years back, there was an assumption that arming yourself gives one a nice peaceful sleep. Guns as we know do not generate peace. As long as there is a presumed or real danger "out there", it would be very difficult for a person to have a complete uninterrupted cycle of sleep. No amount of guns will guarantee anyone of us genuine peace. I have come to believe that neither walls nor a number of guns could guarantee me peace of mind. I've always wondered how many guns can one have in a home before feeling safe? For instance, one may live in a well- built house with steel gates by the entrance, locked well and equipped with monitors, and have several guns locked in the first level of the home and more in the lower part of the building, and may have a dog or dogs trained to attack any intruder; and yet this individual is not able to go through the usual ninety minutes of sleep cycle, or jumps up sometimes in the night because of nightmares. Paranoia can enslave you, and rob you of peace. General anxiety disorders can rob and tax your energy, and as a result you become susceptible to various mental issues. I am not suggesting that walls are bad. As humans we need walls; in our climate we cannot survive without walls. Let me be clear, I am not against walls at all; they are essential and beneficial; winters in Minnesota make one appreciate walls! However, we need to understand that a wall has both negative and positive qualities. My suggestion is that we need to understand that a wall can only protect one to a point. There are many deadly dangers which can disrupt life for which a wall cannot be a solution. Take, for instance, "COVID 19": how high does a wall have to be in order to stop the virus? Or how high a wall can protect one in case of a nuclear war?

Paranoia is not a new phenomenon. It is as old as mankind; it is wrapped in human life itself, and suppression of it tends to fuel more paranoia and disrupt the functions of the human brain such as the central and peripheral nervous systems. The idea that anybody or anything can invade your personal space might make the idea of building walls around the personal space much attractive. Initially we feel much safer and more peaceful when we have control of a situation, and know what comes in and what goes out. Even though the wall locks some people in and keeps others out, symbolically human creativity has found a way to by-pass the wall by having windows to give a sense that one is still part of the larger world.

Another way to look at human relatedness is through the concept of bridges. From a practical sense, the usefulness and function of bridges in our lives remain clear and convincing. Analogously speaking roads become the blood vessels of the country and bridges function as body joints. We know that industrialized countries spend a lot of time and money building modern cities and communities every year. Tiny little communities continue to expand and become towns and cities. Globally, as cities grow larger every few years, the demand for roads becomes prominent, and land communication takes priority. As I previously said, roads and highways become the blood-vessels of the country, and most of these highways and roads are connected by bridges which analogously function as body-joints. Bluntly put, bridges are fundamental and absolutely necessary for any country. They are essential for economy to survive in the 21st century as well as for security reasons. On many occasions, I find myself visualizing America or any other country in the world as a "human body" with various parts functioning in concert. Every part of this large body has a particular and important role to play. One part or a few parts alone cannot guarantee the smooth function of the body. So think of blood vessels; joints, the brain and its intricacy; and so many other parts of the body. Somehow you realize every part of your body is expected to function accordingly for your health. If you ignore one part of your body, I will not be surprised that you may start to feel not very well. When I was young and naïve, I used to think my feet were not as important as my head. Now I know and value every part of my body. I tend to believe that every nation is a "body" which needs to function in concert. The economy of the country depends on functional and efficient transportation. Bridges, highways and ports need to function in concert. My point is, we need to keep in mind that every American has a duty to participate in a nation building. We all live under one canopy as the world. Every nation has an obligation and a duty to see that the next generations prosper and make the world we leave behind better and more prosperous.

In regard to human relatedness, bridges do exactly what walls cannot do. They can serve as links between the "have" and the "have not". They are meant to connect two sides; bridges become the opportunity for humanity to leave the comfortable situation of our homes and neighborhoods for the purpose of reaching the disadvantaged and the needy fellow humans who seem to be isolated and live in remote parts of the world. Today our technology has enabled nations to help and save lives of those whose lands and homes have been destroyed by droughts or, in some cases, by brutal Dictators who constantly pacify the industrialized nations with promises of improving the lives of their citizens. The problems come when we cannot tell the intentions of everyone we encounter. Will those we come to believe are good people, later turn out to be destructive machines? Or will they become friends who will enrich our lives for decades to come? Certainly, there is no way to know for sure. As much as we like our roads and bridges, we know very well that we can never be 100% certain of the intentions of our fellow travelers towards us or towards others. Ironically, people with good intentions can use the roads and cross bridges just as well as people with bad intentions. There lies the risk (and opportunity) of crossing bridges (cultural, economic, religious, racial) to develop relationships with fellow human beings. In recent years and months, our country is experiencing an alarming failure in human relatedness in several areas, including economic and health care disparities, political polarization, racial injustice and inequality, and distrust of police and public officials; however, I still see a glimpse of "hope."

A prime example is that here in Minnesota, after a Policeman squeezed the life out of George Floyd by resting his knee on his neck, there was a public outcry over the injustice done to that man. There were demonstrations not only in Minneapolis, but in many other cities of America protesting the brutality and disregard of human lives, especially of people of color. The public was demanding that fundamental changes are needed in regard to Police attitude toward people of color in this country. People formed a rainbow coalition, with a slogan "**Black Lives Matter**". For several days, there were demonstrations not only in American cities but also overseas. Unfortunately, the KKK, Skin Heads, and white supremacists known as "Hitler's remnants", infiltrated these large groups in American cities, and deceptively marched with everyone else; however, their goals were to set fires on buildings, and destroy businesses in order to demonize these protestors in the eyes of the general public. Sadly, the response from the Trump administration affirmed what had been known for a while based on the President's tone during his political campaign. He literally demonized these protesters, who were demanding justice for people of color by addressing city administrations to stop discrimination and blunt racism. The President trashed and humiliated governors and mayors of certain U.S. cities, saying the reason why protesters were destroying buildings and property, is because these governors and mayors are weak leaders. However, one thing President Trump concealed in his regular tweets is the fact that members of his movement quickly infiltrated these peaceful protesters with a clear intention of demonizing them. These new forms of "Western K.G.B" pretended to be sympathetic and supportive of these peaceful protesters, and faked anger, while their goal was to burn down businesses and police stations under the cover of darkness. While the cities were burning, President Trump was busy fueling members of his organizations through Twitter. These deceptive remnants of Hitler's doctrine infiltrated the country via land and air and caused a lot of damage in several cities of our country. As we all know, there are two sides of everything, namely good and bad; or rather, positive and negative. Our transportation system has both sides. The accessibility of travel made it easier for people with bad intentions to reach their destination to demonize those who were legitimately protesting. This goes to show that, as long as we continue to have Hitler sympathizers in our system, it will continue to be difficult to tell who is a fake and who is a genuine sympathizer.

As if we have not seen enough of chaotic days and weeks in this country, this nation was mysteriously clubbed by a large group of ill-informed citizens who preferred dictatorship to democracy. I suppose these fellow citizens were tired of fair elections. Either they were misled by somebody, or they were just tired of being civilized and having to vote fairly every now and then. They probably thought dictatorship is simple and fair, they probably envy the North Koreans, or the Russians, or Saudis who do not bother with elections every now and then. These groups of Americans wanted to end the system of having elected officials; they wanted to install a King; in other words, they would have preferred to have the title "Your Highness King Trump" to "Mr. President Trump". Therefore, they picked January 6, 2021, to implement their goal and travelled to Washington, D.C., with an intention of bringing the American symbol of democracy to its knees. They forcibly occupied the seat of American government for more than five hours, forcing the law-makers to go into hiding. This mob damaged the building by breaking windows, etc., and some of them beat members of the Capitol police who were trying to protect the building and its legitimate occupants. Later on, it became very clear that this particular mob had the blessing of the President of the United States. For hundreds of years America pursued and upheld the principles of democracy (not always with purity) and never had a sitting President of the United States who supported the dismantling of a government violently. Law-makers were in hiding and remained safe; nevertheless, some lives were lost in the insurrection. This action sent shock waves to American citizens and world leaders, friends and foes alike. These people came to Washington either by driving, flying, train or personal vehicles. They probably used the same roads which any member of the public normally uses to get to places or to work, etc. They crossed bridges like everyone else, and obeyed the traffic lights as any other good citizen. However, their agenda was destructive, but hidden in their minds, only to erupt at the seat of American democracy. This action should remind us all that we cannot take our democratic freedom for granted: please keep in mind that this virus, or the "killer bug" known as "dictatorship," is hovering above Washington, DC, and other democratic countries, looking for a new home. Incidents like this tend to poison the atmosphere and create suspiciousness in communities.

Despite all that, America's role as a beacon of "hope" in a tumultuous world remains intact. Strangely enough, this evil and selfish act (insurrection at the Capitol) might turn out to be a blessing in disguise, or rather a wake-up call. Unfortunately, for some Americans, the reality of WWII remains a fairy tale; however, in my case, the destruction of WWII was not a fairy tale. I was old enough to see young men (older than me) taken away from their families to go fight a war which started in Europe. My father went to the government station every week to pick up an official gazette as one way to track the war activities. I remember those nights when army tanks and trucks travelled close by without lights, and we constantly feared we were not going to be able to see the sunrise. For so many years, Americans have read, heard or seen how other countries experienced *coup d'etat*, but never experienced it in this country. Let us face it, we all know that 'democracy' has fleas on her skin which sometimes prove to be not only a discomfort but potentially a very serious disease if not treated very carefully. However, to use an analogy: if your dog has fleas, I certainly hope you do not kill your dog for that reason. I would hope you find something which will kill the fleas and not the dog. Let us not kill our democracy, instead let us work together to get rid of the fleas. Often, we gave a blind eye to the brutal governments, saying, they will figure that out. I wonder how long the people of North Korea will continue to wait for their leader to loosen his grip? Those nations which are doing business with those oppressive regimes are becoming "enablers," therefore they are guilty. We all share planet "earth"; like it or not, those people who are suffering under brutal and dictatorial governments are our sisters and brothers; they are our neighbors because they belong to the same "quilt". My father used to say, "you are not really safe until your neighbor is safe". It took me years to grasp what he was saying. My comfort and safety are very much relative. For instance, if there is a raging fire in the area driven by strong winds, and people are losing their homes, it would be foolish to ignore the sirens just because the fire is a few miles away from my house. Most of the time the wind does not recognize county lines. If I ignore the evil thing because it is not in my neighborhood today, it might be too late for me to escape once it is all over my property.

Americans love freedom of speech; we love the democratic principle; however, we sometimes forget that "dictatorship" is alive and well. In dictatorial regimes, government is not by the people, for the people, but rather the other way around. Your voice does not count and your life is always dispensable. Democratic societies can become too relaxed, and dismiss the dangers of human freedom just next door. Bluntly speaking, "dictatorship" can join a democratic banquet by wearing a very convincing democratic mask. Unfortunately, President Trump's leadership, knowingly or otherwise, hypnotized millions of people and gave them a feeling of being in wonderland. He promised more than he could deliver. He painted a picture which says: get rich or else you are not an American. A picture which suggested that only a lazy person can be poor in America. He painted an unrealistic and ugly picture of low-income people in America. He attempted to build a psychological wall which keeps only the powerful and rich in; the poor and needy must remain outside. Or to put it differently, his rhetoric created an "us" against "them" mentality. While some citizens bought into this mentality, others found it hard to believe or let alone trust those who display their patriotism by carrying big national flags (sometimes hugging and kissing the flag to demonstrate their patriotism even though in time of war, these same people dodged the draft). Let us be honest, walls are not a solution to our problems. What we need are ideological or philosophical bridges if we are ever going to unify this country which we are truly proud of, a country which our men and women remain willing to defend from inside and outside foes. Patriotism is not found in attacking and conspiring to demolish the seat of American democracy.

It is frightening to find out that the very people who took the oath of office to protect, defend, and preserve the Constitution of United States, willingly conspired with domestic terrorists to crush the symbol of American democracy. This act of terrorism, should be a wake-up call to all democratic nations. Domestic terrorism and foreign terrorism are identical twins. Yet it is much more difficult to fight a terrorist who shares meals with you. My question to my fellow Americans is: what is the difference between those who attacked this country on 9/11, and the recent attackers of January 6, 2021? If you put a loaded gun in the hands of an adolescent who believes that he/she is being bullied by other children at school, and a week later you get a phone call from the Police that your child killed some school mates (using the gun you purchased not too long ago), how would you convince parents of the dead children that you are innocent? Let me put it differently: Bin Laden was in his hiding place when he instructed his loyal disciples to kill as many Americans as possible. The point is, even though Bin Laden was thousand of miles away from America when his followers committed the 9/11 crime, in the eyes of the law he was equally guilty for the crime. Therefore, America was justified not to rest until he was brought to face justice and receive what he had coming. In regard to January 6, 2021, where, then, was the President of United States? What sermon did he preach to his supporters? More importantly, what was the main goal of trashing American Democracy, and what kind of government did the President and his disciples have in mind? I don't know if anybody in that mob had a prototype of a better government than what we have now. May this tragedy inspire us to reach out and build bridges, and lower the height of walls between us, for we are Americans, and we are one in peace time and war time. Evil cannot be stopped by building walls around ourselves, because evil is invisible; it is a virus which attacks the mind and heart of a person. It kills the soul mercilessly. Disagreement among people is inevitable in any democratic society; however, hate, intimidation, prejudice and violence stand as the byproduct of a rotten ego.

During the four years of the Trump administration, our country experienced a typhoon which threatened the existence of a government of the people and for the people. Its gale force winds swept across the land from coast to coast, leaving many Americans in confusion and dismay. The political visibility was dangerously poor, and millions of Americans either gave up hope or felt they were having a bad dream. The barrage of tweets from the administration did not allay Americans' fear; instead, it caused more fear and confusion, and serious suspicion of the administration's intention. At times it felt like "democracy" had been highjacked, leaving millions wondering whether America was still a beacon of hope and freedom in the world. One has to give credit to President Trump for recognizing and acknowledging the imperfections of our government; however, his diagnosis was far off the chart, archaic and dangerous. The greatest danger of his Presidency was not just being miles away from the facts, but rather his deep devotion to his theory which he elevated to a level of dogma through daily tweets. Yes, his presidency was tumultuous most of the time; on the other hand, it was a blessing because it sent a loud siren across America, which woke up millions of people who were in deep sleep. Suddenly, millions were asking: where are we, and where are we going?? Of course, our liberty ship was going straight to dictatorship. Thank God, we woke up before a dreadful ending.

President Trump's administration promised to protect Americans from what he called "thieves, rapists, and drug dealers" from Latin American countries. The administration concluded that American problems were caused by these people from Latin America who sneak into USA and steal jobs from Americans; and to make it worse, they are rapists. This is to say if we build a wall to stop them, Americans will have good jobs and probably better lives.

The Trump administration reached its final hours January 20, 2021, without a single good thing he could show Americans from his wall project. The idea of building a wall the entire length of our southern border was indefensible. We live in a world where wall-building is childish, and not practical. The administration should have considered building a "wall" of cyber security which is capable of stopping the Russians and Chinese from spying on America. We all know the real threat to our country cannot possibly come from job seekers from Latin American countries; nevertheless, these people became scapegoats when things were not going well in our country. Unfortunately, Adolf Hitler used the same sick logic when he wanted to get rid of Germans who happened to be Jews. I do not think we have reached that point yet, but given what the internal mob can do, every decent American should be concerned.

CHAPTER NINE:
MORE BRIDGES, LESS WALLS

The original objectives of bridges were to connect communities, and to make it easier to share technological successes with those who reside in remote areas. Bridges are designed to join or connect those which are apart. Yet there is a problem which in some cases comes with the establishment of bridges. That is, bridges make it much easier for criminals to transfer their commodity anywhere in the country. In regard to commodities, roads and bridges are not the only way common people in business transfer goods and services, but now by the click of the finger people reach beyond their national boundaries. In other words, the term "bridge" has evolved into something faster and invisible. Technology has enabled people to sell and buy merchandise without starting their cars in their garages. People can reach very remote places without ever leaving their houses. The age of the internet has revolutionized the original intent of a "bridge". Technology has shrunk distances, and virtually down-graded the old physical bridges and land roads. By a click of a button, you can either receive or send a very important message which might be used to unify thousands of people, or to send a very divisive and cruel message to thousands or millions of people without ever leaving physical locations. Technology has enabled most of us to connect with our relatives living in other parts of the world without ever leaving present locations. Obviously, when I say "bridge," I am not actually talking about a physical bridge which helps us to cross the rivers etc. to reach our destinations. My use of the term "bridge" is metaphorical. Metaphorically, I am talking about a bridge which is not tangible, and yet very real. This bridge is as old as your first heart-beat.

You cannot survive without it. From the inception of life to the very last breath of life, this bridge remains vital.

For unclear reasons, mankind is designed and created with a very powerful, deep-seated need to interact with that which is its replica. This unconscious urge throws a human soul into a state of restlessness, which means "life" is not in a state of self-contentment. It is for such a reason that life is perpetually searching for the other "self". The fact is, a human soul which is locked in isolation will forever crush the walls and walk the earth, and sail the seas in search of the missing self. To borrow from Rollo May 's Existential Psychology, "The human being lives in 'Umwelt, Mitwelt, and Eigenwelt' simultaneously." (May, Rollo. Contribution of Existential Psychotherapy. In, May, R.; Angel, E.; and Ellenberger, H. F., editors. *Existence: A New Dimension in Psychiatry and Psychology*. 1958, p. 63). Rollo May wrote, "To grasp what it means to exist, one needs to grasp the fact that he might not exist, that he treads at every moment on the sharp edge of possible annihilation and can never escape the fact that death will arrive at some unknown moment in the future" (May, Rollo, 1958, pp. 47-48). In my view, living fully is the ability to establish a bridge between the two realities. It is the capability to acknowledge the existence of both "thesis" and "antithesis" and have a "synthesis" as the ultimate goal. From time to time, we need to remind ourselves that we are neither heavenly angels, nor are we demons. In each of us there are successes, but also failures; hope and despair; happiness and sadness; health and sickness; love and hate; and life and death. We are all of that, yet we are not split personalities. We have poor people in this global canopy, but we also have rich people. Neither side can ignore the other. A civilized society has to build a bridge between the rich and the poor. It is inhumane to isolate a segment of a population, or blow up the bridge of communication, just because of poverty or wealth. Believe it or not, the wealthy people, just as the poor people, will reach the final exit, and none will be able to say a word in a closed coffin.

Those who spend their entire lives in seclusion in the name of peace and tranquility, are a self-imprisoned group of people. These are people who believe that anybody who is not like them, or who is at the bottom step of the stratification ladder, must be evil or lazy. Rich and industrialized nations should be very careful in how they interact with developing and poor nations. It would be wise for the rich nations to coach and nurture the poor countries, for in that way poor countries can build their own economies, and would interact with other nations not as "beggars" but rather as "partners". We need to learn how to strengthen bridges between genders, cultures, young and old. We need to narrow the gap and build bridges between liberals and conservatives, between large corporations, financial institutions, and those who live from paycheck to paycheck without the ability to invest anything for retirement. How do we justify the overwhelming wealth in the hands of very few, while the number of homeless people is steadily rising in our cities? Are we really as civilized as we claim to be? Certainly, how we define "civilization" remains controversial and illusive. This term has been used to differentiate those countries with more military, economic, and technical power from those countries which find themselves on the periphery of these things. Linguistically, the definition of "civilization" is very much subjective. If we are to take a non-biased definition, we will soon find out that no nation (so far) in the world has even come close to true meaning of civilization. If we turn our attention to evolution, and see how far we have come, we will have to admit that, "humanity" and all that we label as "civilization" is still at infancy stage. In regard to our behavior toward each other, I am sorry to say we are not any farther from the brutes in Serengeti National Park. In many cases those animals get along better than we do as human beings. To my knowledge there is no country in the world which has truly reached the level or the status of civilization. By this I mean a country with concrete evidence of a high level of intellectual, social or cultural development. I mean a country where the big fish spares the life of the little fish.

On several occasions I visited National Parks both in Tanzania and Kenya. I observed elephants staying together, and in their midst one can spot a matriarch leader. Lions, zebras, impala, hippos and many other types of animals seem to have organizational skills. Some of these animals are constantly in a defensive mode. At times I ask myself: what is the difference between those animals in the Serengeti and human beings? For instance, I can understand why zebras are afraid of lions, and why impala prefer to stay in open areas. These poor animals are constantly watching and moving around for fear of predators in the area. As a Maasai, I learned that a lion will kill for food. Mankind kills his/her own kind for what purpose? We spend years writing volumes in an attempt to justify our wars and our weapons which are intended to kill and destroy not elephants but our own kind. Mankind has been fighting wars for centuries, and still no lasting peace in sight. The painful truth is: wars were never designed to forge peace. Our country and Russia hold approximately 90% of nuclear weapons. Can we say truthfully, we now feel peaceful? Or can we say the industrialized and rich countries are civilized? The answer to that question is: "we are neither civilized nor peaceful."

War can only give birth to war. We have plenty of examples in that regard. Look at Iraq, Afghanistan, Libya, Syria, Yemen, and Somali; do we see or hear any birth of "peace" in those countries? These conflicts compounded and complicated the already human tragedy. How did all these wars begin? What constructive role did industrialized countries play in these countries? Did our involvement foster peace and constructive negotiations among the local leaders? I am sorry to say, many times the involvement of the industrialized countries worsens the already fractured countries. We saw that during and after the war in Iraq. That war (in Iraq) did not build a bridge between the Shia and the Suni. Our involvement in the Middle East did not generate peace. What about the wars Israel and her neighbors fought, off and on, for years? Realistically, can the citizens of these countries claim they finally got peace? So, when you hear the word: "peace," what are you thinking and feeling? Is peace a wishful thinking? Is humanity capable of forging peace? How do we define peace, or do we have a universal definition of "peace"?

It would be disingenuous on my part if I did not state my position in regard to the nature of a "wall". I previously alluded to the principal idea that the term "bridge" is metaphorical. I pointed out the usefulness of it and also the problems which come with it. The term "wall" is no exception. My discussion of the "wall" is metaphorical. The wall which is built by using bricks and cement or mud, as long as it meets the objectives of the builder, is a good wall. This kind of wall is stationary and probably reliable. But that type of wall is actually a prototype of the invisible wall in a human psyche. The invisible wall in the human psyche is not stuck in one place or time. Normally it is not static; it reacts to changes within and without. It responds to the present situation and takes the role of a "protector". It is very much protective of the ego. The problem with this, is the fact that it can misread the external message directed to the ego.

Our country has been at odds with Russia for years, and we believe we have the most powerful defense in case of Russia's aggression. I assume Russia is also very sure it can defend its nation against any outside enemy. In regard to West/East relations, we still have a huge problem. We just do not trust each other's motives, and we actually intensify our spying activities with an intention of destabilizing each other's government. As a result, we spend so many resources preparing ourselves in case the other side decides to attack first. Unfortunately, the Russian regime has been very successful in eating lunches or suppers with the Western leaders without being exposed. In regard to West/East relations, the century-old question remains: When will East and West achieve "peace"? Can we build a wall high enough which can protect us from outside aggression? No! we cannot, because the disease is already in our hearts and minds. However, we should not spend too much time feeling bad for our inability to prevent a tragedy. In my opinion, since the enemy is not out there, but rather is sharing our bedrooms with us, we should start the process of building a humane society by taking baby steps towards reconciliation via taking personal responsibility. Uniting America should be our first priority. We should remember that harmonious relationship does not come out of arguments and finger pointing, but rather by sincere repentance, and admission of wrong doing. Let us not forget that the oppressor also needs to be freed from the desire to oppress others. Similarly, the oppressed need to be freed from the desire to celebrate the humiliation of the oppressor. Jesus said: "pray for your enemies." He did not say wait until they stop being your enemies, then pray for them, but rather, pray for them so they can turn away from their demonic ways.

A few years ago a graduate student who was frustrated by my "deep seated hope" asked me why I continue to hope in the midst of a chaotic situation? I quickly responded, because I come from Africa. Looking puzzled, he said, "so what?" At this point I asked him if he ever heard of Nelson Mandela, to which he responded, "of course! He was the first black President of South Africa." I asked him why his Presidency was historical. That he was not able to explain, how that came about. I decided to help him understand how South Africa came to be under the white government for hundreds of years even though the majority population of South Africa has always been Africans. Historically the South Africa natives were kind and friendly enough to have accommodated the Dutch merchants (in 1602 A.D) who built the Cape Town settlement, to enable them to repair and resupply their ships. Eventually the guests turned into an aggressive and land-snatching force. To put it into a contemporary thinking, I asked my graduate student to imagine a couple who were born and had been in the state of Montana all their lives (their grandparents had had the land for many years, this is the fourth generation). Their home was not very far away from the highway. As good farmers they always left the yard light on during the nights. This area was not heavily populated; one could drive some miles without seeing a home. Winter can be punishing, beyond anybody's imagination. This particular night, the snow came down mercilessly. The snow, mixed with strong winds, covered the highway, and whoever was on the road got stranded. One particular family stopped their car just before it went into a ditch. They were scared because the wind kept on relentlessly, and they lost a sense of direction. They decided to get out of the car to see if they could detect any sign of life. As they walked away from the car which was being covered by the blowing snow, they saw a flickering little light at a distance. For a while they argued among themselves whether it was a light or a star in the horizon.

The family decided to follow that dimmed light; as they walked, they lost sense of the whereabouts of their car; however, they also knew going back to that car was going to be nothing but suicidal. They walked toward the flickering light across the fields, and the longer they walked the weaker and colder they felt. They felt the more they walked, the nearer the light got. The closer they got, the more desperate they got. Sure enough, it was a yard light, and it was a home! These strangers who were very cold and tired when they got closer to the gate, started calling, "Please, is anybody here? Please help us! We are cold and tired! Please help us, we are freezing!" Fortunately, the old man heard somebody calling for help. He woke up his wife, saying there are people outside the gate calling for help. She got up too and woke up the rest of the family as they were debating whether it was safe to let strangers in the house in the middle of the night. They opened the gate and let the pathetic-looking strangers walk in, and immediately gave them dry blankets and made them some coffee and food since they were hungry and tired. The host family decided to give up their bedroom for that night, and the owner and his wife went into the basement where they have a nice cozy little bed, normally used by friends of their children whenever they spend a night or "sleep over". These strangers were so grateful, and thankful that this farm family saved them. The host family members were touched by the words of appreciation from the unexpected guests. The farmer's family felt so good about their decision to help save lives of people they did not know anything about. All went well until the morning: when the farmer's family woke up, they found their guests eating breakfast luxuriously, with a loaded gun on the table. The host family was stunned and confused; they thought it was a sick joke. When they made an attempt to get to their bedrooms, their guest pulled a gun and led them to the basement telling them, "From now on you will serve us and do whatever we tell you; if you obey and be good enough, we will give you food or any basic essentials. If you disobey, we will kill you." The farmer and his family went from being owner of their ancestral land to slaves of the invaders who snatched away the rights of this family who had opened their gate and their door out of compassion.

Similarly, the Dutch sailors were stranded near the Cape of Good Hope; they needed to repair their ships, and rest, before they embarked on their long journey. The land was occupied by natives of South Africa. The Zulu people (who were known to be warriors), whether out of curiosity or just kindness, did let the Dutch sailors and their friends venture into the Zulu land. Unfortunately, the Zulu were not able to realize the sailors' intention of colonialism until it was too late. The owners of that beautiful land became slaves of the strangers for many centuries. In this case the act of compassion produced nothing but regrets. The story about the winter in Montana bluntly portrays how the Dutch invaders got into South Africa around 1602. The Dutch invaded South Africa, and took the tribal chiefs by surprise. For centuries they convinced the other colonizers that the south of the African continent was their homeland. In other words, they claimed to be natives. Despite all this painful history which is replicated in many parts of the world, I am amazed that natives of the invaded lands are consistently forgiving and generous. When will the colonizers of these lands ever apologize to the descendants of the legitimate natives? It is not a matter of money, but a moral and sincere apology would heal most of the historical wounds of slavery and humiliation that the natives of these lands experienced.

I think our country can learn a few good things from the "Truth and Reconciliation Commission" (TRC) devised by President Nelson Mandela of South Africa after apartheid ended. President Mandela took over leadership of a country which for years had the worst human rights record in Africa. The TRC shocked a lot of people, and took many by surprise. The core intention of the TRC was not designed or built on the notion of "an eye for an eye". Mandela knew that the oppressor (white government) would have never been able to pay back or mend or give back the innocent countless lives they destroyed for hundreds of years. He wanted the heirs of the oppressive government to tell the oppressed the truth (the whole truth): how they mistreated the natives of South Africa, why they massacred even school children. The parents of those children in Soweto who were massacred by the government forces wanted closure by confronting the killers. They wanted to know where the mass graves were so they could try to find something of these children, such as clothes, shoes or anything tangible to connect them with their children who had been brutally murdered. They did not want to hear more baseless reasons and justification given by the Apartheid government every year; they wanted to start a new page of life with a clear understanding of why they were brutalized by the oppressive government. From that point on, the relatives of the dead wanted to continue moving forward to fulfill hopes and dreams of their loved ones. Prior to the establishment of Truth and Reconciliation, I was lucky to meet Archbishop Desmond Tutu in Wisconsin; he later was named by Nelson Mandela as the chair of the TRC. Furthermore, a wonderful friend of our family, Bishop Patrick Matolengwe of South Africa, served in the TRC. The TRC was a safe channel for both parties to meet and vent out what was behind the killing of innocent people, and a place where those who allowed themselves to be used as "killing machines" of the white government, acknowledged their misled and blind loyalty which led them to kill innocent citizens. After admitting such destructive attitude and actions, the oppressor then faced the victim's family to determine the outcome, and anything else for the family to have closure.

Even though here in America we may not be able to emulate the exact structure of South Africa's Truth and Reconciliation Commission, we can still establish something like that as a starter. If we ever think of having something similar to TRC, we would have to select experts from various groups, such as religious leaders, constitutional law experts; psychologists and sociologists.

The oppressed groups in this country who have been discriminated against and oppressed by the system based on skin color, gender, ethnicity, or country of origin would benefit from a round table confessional meeting with oppressor groups. The outcome of these meetings would be determined by an America Truth and Reconciliation Commission (ATRC).

The committee should be structured in such a way that both the oppressed and the oppressor are instructed to tell the truth (the whole truth) about the oppression and brutal tactics the white government used for years to suppress Africans in this country. The heart and engine of this group should be "tell the truth, the whole truth, and let the oppressed vent and both (oppressed and oppressor) find ways to have a new beginning. The struggle during the Civil Rights Movement exposed the United States; it undressed the U.S. persona for the whole world to see. This generation has an obligation to heal the wounds and mend the bridges between the privileged and the marginalized. Americans need to acknowledge that our past is nothing to brag about. We need to acknowledge our weaknesses, but be bold enough to correct them. We still treat Native Americans as aliens from somewhere else. An African American is still treated as 3/5 of a human being. The law of the land is written to protect the white race, and penalize the people of color. Because of my skin I am guilty until proven innocent. Those who are white are innocent until proven guilty. Black children still run away from law enforcement officers, while white children will feel safe when the police show up in the neighborhood. Financial institutions are reluctant to lend money to those who happen to be black, and most of the time those blacks who happen to be educated live under suspicion, or make people's heads turn, followed with a whisper, "how did he get that education?". If you are black and have a decent house and live in a small town, people assume you must have gotten the money from a shady business. If you are poor and live in the depressed neighborhood, then you are lazy, and probably dependent on government money. And then we wonder why black children grow up with a low self-esteem or in some cases a low self- concept.

In regard to the formation of the TRC as previously mentioned, the committees were structured in such a way that both the oppressed and the oppressor were instructed to tell the truth (the whole truth) about the oppression and brutal tactics the white government used for years to suppress Africans in their own country. President Nelson Mandela did an excellent job engineering that approach. The mandate was, "tell the truth, the whole truth, and let the other side decide and weigh your honesty. Families of the victims listened to the confessions of the oppressors and their admission of wrong doing. At the end there was a chance for a new chapter in South Africa. To ensure that the backbone of apartheid is dismantled forever, the government created programs to help the segments of the population which were oppressed for years by the laws of apartheid system, to join in the effort of building a new democratic South Africa. In our case (present America), it is not going to be easy to believe that promises from the European Americans are going to satisfy people of color, particularly African Americans and Native Americans. Yet we cannot wait for another country to help us start fixing the bridges between us, bridges that many believed would never be built, because of racism and discrimination. Americans need to acknowledge the urgency of a sincere dialogue followed by actions, before it is too late. America has lost moral leadership in the world, however that can only be gained after we restore dignity to our people right here at home. We are at a point where dictators around the world are not ashamed to display their brutality, for they instantly know our house is not in order. I am concerned we are running out of time to open dialogue groups around the country. We need to realize that our enemy is with us all the time; the hate and discrimination which is displayed in higher sectors of the government, and social gatherings, has been saturating many parts of our lives. It would not be an exaggeration to say your enemy knows your heart-beats. The enemy is constantly building a wall between you and the other person you encounter in your life journey.

No country (knowingly) goes out of its way to welcome people with evil intentions. Yes, as a civil nation, we communicate with anybody who is willing to communicate with us, but there is no way to know for sure the deep intentions of our guests. This is to say, the bridge of communication and interaction is open and can be used by anybody. The day you entered this world was also the beginning of facing your vulnerability and the reality that nothing is 100% certain in life. Today you may be very healthy and feel very safe; however, you have no guarantee for how long. Those people who got killed by Timothy McVeigh when he bombed the Alfred P. Murrah Federal Building in Oklahoma City were taken by a tragic surprise. That single violent person destroyed the lives of many innocent people. McVeigh burned down the dreams of many he had never met. He stole their hopes, and their tomorrows. Out of that horrific incident, American counter culture of the far right gained prominence, when it was revealed that the main actor of that day was a member of the far-right group of Americans who boast as patriots and true Americans. The point is, the idea or a belief that the enemy is that new face in your block or city, does not go very far. Horrible massacres in schools, night clubs, even places of worship were, and are, not being carried out by those across our borders, but rather by those with whom we share bread and butter in our own cities and rural areas. Let us not forget that the worst enemy is (in many cases) not outside your house, but rather the one you would have never suspected in your life. Evil thrives in the hearts of people, not in plants or rocks.

Selfishness and self-centeredness drive people to do awful things. Years back, people feared that Russians or other foreign powers might invade us; now those foreign powers do not have to invade, because we are killing ourselves. The destructive attitude does not dwell and thrive outside the human brain, rather it dwells and thrives there (in the brain), undetectable until it is too late to stop. Fear of other people, or rather fear of people you have never met, can enslave you or lock you in the closet for the rest of your life here on earth. The assumption that every new face out there is a sign of danger can drive one into hypervigilance and delusion. In this world absolute safety may not be attainable; however, we have to be courageous enough to extend a hand shake to those who are willing to dialogue with us. Of course, you can correctly argue that in today's technological world, one can live happily without anybody around. That is, if you are rich enough, you can use a helicopter to come and go places or use drones to deliver groceries right to your door. In this way you can convincingly argue that feeling and being happy does not have anything to do with human relationships. For those reasons you may not want to have a bridge which connects you with the rest of the population. You believe that weak-minded people are the ones who need someone to lean on; while you may definitely feel sorry for them, you would not have anything to do with them.

Fear of domination, attack, or being invaded by those outside our social circles, leads to paranoia; as a result, we demonize the outer group, which of course becomes a pretext for war. As human beings, we are always going to look different, walk, talk, eat, laugh, cry, and think differently, and yet these differences should not be the principal reason for killing each other. We lack the conceptual ability of viewing differences among us as complementary rather than a threat. Our feeble egos sound the alarm whenever we encounter the "otherness". We convince ourselves that anything outside our "in-group" is dangerous and should be avoided, or better yet eliminated. We foolishly alienate and separate others in pursuit of peace and happiness. Yet we never feel peaceful and courageous enough to extend a hand-shake to those at our door steps, or those who happen to have a different perspective of life. The fear of the new situation, or rather the fear of losing control, tends to dominate us so much to a point where we actually dogmatize and theologize the hate of those who are not like us. We go as far as recruiting God to be on our side and fight on our behalf. Some religious leaders surprisingly become lobbyists hard at work winning God's approval for our behavior. Our attempt to anthropomorphize God is at a point where some of us do actually invoke His name every time we kill or blow ourselves up. This means we are not interested in a God who does not take sides. God is being pulled in every direction. In other words, the Creator is being asked to take sides. The question in my mind or in your mind as well is this: who created the other people? I personally believe that God created all people, created the universe, created the visible and invisible; I believe God is above time and space, and creation cannot dictate or control His will.

In 1987 I visited the USSR, and had an opportunity to visit a mass grave in Leningrad (about 120,000 were buried there as a result of the two- and-a-half year siege of Leningrad). During that time, the Leningraders ate almost anything they were able to chew, such as paper or boiled wall paper scraped off walls because its paste was said to contain potato flour. More than a million Leningraders died during the German siege. Since I was the only person from Africa at the mass grave site, and who happened to have lost close neighbors in that war, I was asked to lay flowers on that massive grave in memory of the many Africans who lost their lives in that senseless war. As I was laying the flowers on that grave, I had a prayer in my heart and hoped that such a mass killing shall not be repeated. With a puzzled feeling, I remember muttering in my native language saying, "how many more wars shall be fought before mankind can attain peace?" I do not believe I am any closer to the answer today than I was thirty-six years ago. At times, a little voice tells me, "Wars will be fought as long as women have children". However, that is simplistic because that sounds like saying, if only women stop having children, men would stop making wars. This thought is not practical and not realistic; moreover, it gives an impression that women do not make wars, which is not true; also, it portrays women as the principal actors and men as innocent, which also is not true. In the Old Testament, Adam made a blunt attempt to blame Eve for the trouble they found themselves in. God did not let him off the hook. Both (man/woman) are capable of going left or right or, to put it differently, they are both capable of loving or hating. Throughout history the world has had kings and queens; some of these rulers have been kind to their subjects, and some have been punitive, regardless.

CHAPTER TEN:
RICH CORPORATIONS FEED ON GHETTOS

It was early in the evening; all the cattle, sheep and donkeys were all sleeping safely in the "kraal" (engang o nkishu) The stars were bright, and the moon shone majestically that night. I remember someone telling us boys the following story: Once upon a time there lived a lion and his wife near the edge of the forest. This couple had two cubs years back, but then the cubs grew up and left the area to establish their families. This means it had been many years since this old couple had seen or taken care of a little one. The old couple did not do much other than hunt smaller animals for food. They spent most of their afternoons sleeping under some big trees in the area. Other animals were busy doing what normally animals do. Those who enjoyed fruit spent most of their time around trees which produce fruit. One morning on their way to hunting, this couple saw a small lion cub near some shrubs distressfully moving, and appearing to be very weak. They went closer to check on this poor thing; sure enough, they recognized to whom it belonged; however, they could not find the mother (lioness) or the father. Apparently, they both had been shot dead by hunters. This couple felt sad to see the little one suffering without any help. They looked at each other, and they decided to rescue this little cub. Then they realized it had been a long time since they had had cubs of their own; besides, the lion never really had had patience with little ones. At that point both of them decided to call a big meeting of all the animals in the area to see if anyone would like to be hired to take care of this cub. Many animals came to the meeting, but they did not want to take the job because of the fear of the lion. They only came to the meeting out of respect and fear of what would happen if the lion and lioness found out that they did not attend that meeting. The older couple took the cub home and attempted to feed him, but things were not going very well. A few days later, candidates for the job came for interview. The whole week went by without a suitable candidate. This couple did not want to hire anyone but a vegetarian, because in that way, they could be sure the meat they would provide for the cub would not be eaten by the "nanny". Most of the animals who depend on meat for food, did not bother to apply. However, a fox found a way to get the job. He went out in a forest and killed a monkey, and skinned it very carefully. He made a suit out of this skin, something which fitted him nicely. He put it on and walked through the forest. Monkeys treated him just like other monkeys. He practiced a few monkey-tricks, and certainly all the animals he met on the way to the lion's home believed he was a monkey.

On his way there the "monkey" (fox) practiced sobbing and crying as if his heart was so touched by the death of the parents of this poor cub, and also touched by the kindness and generosity of this old couple. During the interview, he faked tears and claimed he happened to be an orphan, too. He said that his parents were killed when he was very young, and he had to be raised by a non-relative. The lion couple read him the requirements for the job, one being that they will supply the food, and they would expect the "nanny" to feed the cub properly. The fox agreed and the old couple arranged to deliver meat every morning. They showed the fox (who pretended to be a monkey) a nice hut nearby, where he was going to stay with the cub. The old couple kept their word. They delivered meat every morning at the door steps, and the Nanny supposedly fed the cub. After a few weeks, the old couple wanted to know the condition of the cub. One morning as they were delivering the meat, they wanted to go in to see the cub, but the Nanny forbade them, saying the cub had a sort of flu and they should stay away until the situation changes. The couple complied; however, they continued to drop off the meat at the door, and the Nanny was always there to pick it after they left as a way to avoid any more questions. After a month or so, the couple demanded to see the cub, but when they got there with the meat, there was a big sign hanging on the door saying: STAY AWAY! DO NOT COME IN. IT IS HIGHLY CONTAGIOUS. From a distance, the couple asked: HOW IS THE CUB? The Nanny shouted back with a little bit of rough voice, "THE CUB IS DOING FINE, EVERYTHING IS UNDER CONTROL". The old couple left. Two days later a Hare walked by and saw that big sign. He wanted to find out what was all that about. He went in calling: Hallo, hallo, is anybody here? He went in and what he saw was shocking. He walked in and saw what looked like a monkey eating meat (which was unheard of). He looked and saw a lion cub tied to a post, very skinny and without enough strength to break loose. Immediately the fox grabbed the Hare by the neck, threatening to break his neck if he ever told anybody what he saw. The poor Hare, fighting for air, managed to say: "I don't know what you are talking about, I did not see anything because I am blind. I know I should not have gotten out of my house, because I am lost and I do not know how I got here". Hearing that, the fox threw the Hare outside, saying, "I am sorry. I did not know you are blind." The Hare took off running and shouting, "I saw a monkey eating meat!" Fortunately, at that very time, the lion had called a meeting to warn all the animals that there is a disease in the area and they should be very careful. As the lion was speaking, the Hare sped right into the meeting saying, "You cannot believe it, I saw a monkey eating meat. This monkey has a little cub who is so skinny tied to the post. I had never seen a monkey eating meat". At that moment everybody stopped talking; they all stared at the Hare. You could hear a pin drop. The older couple looked at each other, and stood up and said, "That is the Nanny who is taking care of the little orphan. Is that why she kept us at bay? Did she turn to be a beef eater? We are all going to that place and she will have to explain." The entire group of animals followed the Hare right to the hut where the fake monkey was eating meat. The lion roared angrily and knocked the hut down and freed the poor skinny cub. The lioness grappled the fake monkey by the neck, and pulled down the monkey's skin, and sure enough, it was a fox wearing a monkey suit, and it was a male not a female fox . He got the maximum penalty.

The story was told to us many years ago, thousands of miles from here; yet it never lost its teaching intention. Cheating and taking advantage of less able among us, did not only permeate the wild kingdom, but it certainly found a home in the heart of our civilization. The story tells me the fox is still eating the beef which was intended for the poor and skinny cub. We are all familiar with a trend in which large corporations build huge and highly sophisticated businesses in very poor neighborhoods, and in this way the corporation gets a tax break. The citizens near these centers do not benefit, because the companies hire people from outside these poor communities while at the same time claiming their presence in these poor neighborhoods is improving the lives of people in those neighborhoods. Commonly these companies work out details with local leaders, telling them that the corporation is going to be good for the economy of the area, and yet the entire system is staffed by outsiders who drive in to work in the mornings and drive away from there before sunset. For the corporation, it is a win, win situation. Emptying waste baskets, and vacuuming floors, does not boost the economy of these marginalized areas of our cities. If the government is trusting the financial centers and corporations to help improve the economy of the poor working Americans, I seriously think it is like trusting the fake monkey to feed the starving "cub". This is not a general indictment of every large corporation in our country, because we all know some companies which make an effort to lift up the neglected neighborhoods. Unless the industrialized countries come up with meaningful and practical plans that give voice to the marginalized citizens of these old and deteriorating cities, I certainly believe the "fox in the monkey skin" will continue to get fat, and the poor little cub will continue to starve and eventually die in his sleep. I believe that those who are caught in a cycle of poverty, somehow can still be partners in any plan of rescuing them from their starvation and indignity.

Chapter Ten: Rich Corporations Feed on Ghettos

America is one of the richest countries, and one of the leading indus-trialized countries in the world, and it has the resources and the manpower to keep it that way for a long time. However, we also know that the streets of our cities are crowded by homeless people who are never sure where their next meal will come from. The number of homeless people has been growing steadily, and other than trading charges, no one seems to have a solution that would satisfy the "poor" and the "rich" simultaneously. As a result, the rich blame the poor for being poor, saying they put themselves in that position, therefore let them work their way out of it. In other words, they made their own bed, therefore they should sleep in it. In addition to being labeled as a "lazy bunch," poor people are viewed as being happy in their poverty. There is an assumption that these poor people would not be happy if they were to be rich. Of course, we all know that is a stereotype which is used to exon-erate the rich and justify the meager salaries the low-income people have to be content with. There are those both in the Congress and the Senate of the United States, who were terrified by any effort to help low-income Americans to be able to feed their families or pay their electric bills in the middle of the COVID-19 pandemic. These fat rich cats are willing to oppose any move to help disadvantaged Americans get on their feet. They are literally thrilled to block any bill which would raise the minimum wage to $15 an hour for those hard-working Americans. The same lawmakers would not take a cut when it comes down to their own income. Therefore, ask yourself, what is the difference between these lawmakers and the sleek "fox" in our story? The sad thing is, we have a hard time learning the naked truth of life itself, meaning: "all you collected in your life, and all the power you garnered in your career, will not stand against your last visitor in life: the permanent embarkation". You may say the loved one will honor your will, but you need to remember: the loved one will do what they see fit. You may frown in your grave but you cannot take them to court. Those you treated like garbage will exit like everyone else, and that is why we say: death is the leveler. The powerful and the beggar here on earth, shall bow and salute the disembarkation of this life equally, and no judicial court can overturn the verdict.

This simple stereotype, "a lazy bunch," does give birth to discrimination. Unfortunately, in many cases those who find themselves in a receiving line every year, end up developing a very sad attitude and belief that poverty is their destiny. Because of many years of being treated as "rejects" of society, and many years of failing to capture a bit of prosperity in the richest country in the world, they finally adapted and accepted that "poverty" is part of their nature: it is innate, or to put it in other words, it is God's will. Some say poverty is a curse which people of color in our country have to be content with. Generation after generation of being treated like a "disease" of the society, drove the "working poor" of this rich society to habituate their poverty and conclude that they were born poor, and they will die poor. The mental adaptation of "poverty" and "not good enough" had been infused in minds of those whose ancestral history points to Africa, or Latin American countries. Over the three hundred years of indoctrination of that belief of "low self-image," the system managed to create a whole new generation which is neither African nor European. They did not choose to be born here; they found themselves here, and this is the only home they know and will ever know. If anybody is an "American" in a true sense of the word, these despised and brutalized citizens, who have been laughed at by the upper class and heartless politicians (who unfortunately never learned much from Hitler's narcissistic behavior) are true Americans. Unfortunately, those born with silver spoons in their mouths forget that these despised people whose ancestors worked and died penniless, building the infrastructure of this land, have earned the right to be treated and respected as true Americans. To put it psychologically: it is not the gravity of the abusive language which kills the human spirit, but rather the repetitiveness of the abusive language which suffocates the human heart. For instance, if you grow up in a community which relentlessly treats and views you as garbage, there is a great probability that your brain will adapt and act according to your new "identity". Your brain will adopt this "new normal" and fight against any treatment contrary to what you have been socialized in or rather hypnotized in.

The aforementioned story about the sleek fox should not be something to laugh about, or dismiss as just a story about animals in the jungle. This sort of behavior has been going on in many industrialized countries, especially here in America. Our government is very much aware of what the corporations are doing to fatten themselves at the expense of working low-income people in this country. Those in government leadership are supposed to be fair-minded and inclusive in their policies regarding: (a) education for all of our citizens who are eager to better themselves; (b) creation of better paying jobs in this country, rather than rushing out of the country looking for cheap labor in poor dictatorial countries (because doing such a thing is not only robbing the vulnerable poor, but is also immoral), and (c) distribution of health care in this country, which needs not only a patching job, but rather a complete overhaul. The way I see it, our health care is only for the middle class and the very rich. These two groups are the only ones which can afford adequate health care. The Affordable Care Act only scratched the surface of the problem. If there is disparity in our country, it certainly is evident in health care. To put it bluntly, without adequate health insurance which includes coverage for medications, the rich and the millionaires would be the only people who would comfortably afford medications and other health care. The pharmaceutical companies are indirectly deciding who is to live and who is to die. For example, how many working-class people, and retired teachers, carpenters or police officers can afford one "Advair Diskus 250/50" for $433.33 every month? Those suffering from "asthma" need this medication. The problem is, if you do not have the money, you might attempt to skip some days, which of course might put your life in danger. To put it bluntly: the pharmaceutical and health insurance companies do have the last word, and the law makers in our nation's capital know that. Russia and the former "Soviet Block" countries have their system which not many people from the West would like to have; nevertheless, they do not parade themselves as democratic at all; the system is concealed under the arm-pits of whoever is the "dictator". In this way citizens are not expecting much from those who are sitting in the driver's seats of their governments. European countries are colorful, because some have excellent health benefits, and some are not so good; however, most of them keep their citizens at the center of any discussion which has to do with their health care. Some have a concept of socialism, but such a socialism is miles away from what we know as "soviet socialism". In general, one will find that most European governments take the health of their citizens very seriously, and the elderly are not simply tolerated (as we tend to do in our country) but appreciated and respected by the system. I have been in several European countries in my life time, and I was impressed how these small countries run inclusive governments. The voices of the little people can be heard by politicians and civil servants without exception. Union workers are not viewed as a threat to the nation, but rather as a necessary function of a working nation. Yes, "labor unions" are very popular in European countries, and they are not viewed as enemies of the governments, but as an important link of a healthy government. From time to time, you may see a disagreement between the government in office and the labor union, but at no time does the government go out of its way to try to break the labor union. Such a situation is what I term, a bump in the road. There could be shouts and loud voices, but never forget: it is just a "family discussion;" it is not a divorce at all.

America can do better, because we are not only a large country but also a very rich country. The multiculturalism in our country fails to thrive because the "greedy rich" and the "racists" got married. The greedy rich are paranoid, and fearful of being robbed by the poor people who are everywhere, staring at the rich folks as if they are going to suck all the oxygen out of them. At the same time the racist politicians are busy writing laws to either incarcerate the law-breakers or strip the basic human rights of those who do not look like "our type". So here we see "Adolf Hitler" theory and belief coming alive in our 21st century. Remember, Hitler blamed the German Jews for the financial problems of the country, propagating that the permanent solution for Germany was to extract them by all means possible, which included the brutal gas chambers.

In the 21st century we should have better choices in dealing with our economic problems. I dare to say we have everything we need to solve our poverty problems, but unfortunately, we clearly lack the "will" to do so. We seriously lack the basic knowledge which every good farmer has. For instance, does a farmer withhold his seeds of last year's harvest in a storage bin because of the unpredictability of the rain, saying, "unless I am convinced the rain will be here on time, I will not put my seeds in the ground, hoping for the rains to come. It is too much of a risk"? I will definitely tell you this: experienced farmers would not go that route. I am highly certain that any experienced farmer knows there is a certain amount of unpredictability in farming, because weather changes without prior warning. A serious farmer (like my late father-in law) combines two major things, or rather two deep-seated fundamentals in his life, namely: **hope,** which is wrapped in **faith,** which as a result gives him a sense of peace that crops are going to grow in due time. As a result, he does not have to get up in the middle of the night to check if the seeds are germinating or not. In my father-in-law's farming years, three major principles worked in concert: hope, faith and peace. I am not sure whether he was always aware of those three principles of life, nevertheless, the function of that trinity was obvious to me. As I observed him for a number of years, he simply knew that a person who is afraid of taking a calculated risk, may not last very long in farming. Of course, there are losses and gains in anything we do in our lives; whether we farm or immerse ourselves in other professions, we should keep in mind that losses and gains are in the cards. Our country is able to eradicate poverty, and reduce homelessness in our cities and raise the standard of living, by raising the minimum wage to a living wage, as an incentive to get able bodies to support themselves or their families. Believe me, no parent wants to be a beggar, and no child would be happy having a parent who has to beg for bread or a glass of milk every week. It is humiliating and distressing, and it kills the ego of that child who constantly worries if there will be supper in the evening, or a glass of milk in the morning. We blindly and foolishly expect these children to thrive and excel in school. America is not only the most powerful country in the world, but also the richest industrialized country in the world, and yet we lack a will to eradicate poverty which grows bigger and larger every year. We are not only a rich and smart nation, but also powerful militarily; however, we lack the "will" to eradicate poverty and hunger in the very heart of our cities.

As a nation, on the outside we look powerful and big; however, inside we are infested with starvation, poor health, and defeated egos. In short, America has become a caste society. Those on the top get all the oxygen and a good view of the world, and those on the bottom are gasping for air. I thought we (Americans) were supposed to be the light and good example in the world, or do you suppose the battery needs to be re-charged? Whatever happened to religion? Where is the moral compass? Television has become a battlefield. Preachers are constantly using television to lure more people by promising them that they know exactly what God expects of them. The only problem is, these preachers are much richer than the viewers who, most of the time, empty pockets and deprive themselves of life essentials (such as decent food, a decent place to call home, necessary health care) while the preachers have beautiful homes, expensive means of transportation, and Churches (meeting halls) that resemble movie-theaters. It would be a relief to see these preachers help and teach their viewers how to improve their lives, so they do not have to live in poverty. Believe me, there is nothing wrong in television preaching, however the danger comes when these preachers become very wealthy while the viewers who support them remain poor the rest of their lives. I would suggest that a healthy person can hear and understand the sermon better than a person who is hungry and worrying how to pay a heating bill or rent. It would be nice to see these wonderful preachers visit the ghettos of our cities, and listen to those people's fears and hopes before delivering sermons. Connect with those who have been neglected by the system: do what Christ did; go to the people, rather than people coming to you. Yes, we live in a world where some have more than they need, and some people have just basics. I am not suggesting or insinuating that the very rich in our society are evil blood suckers. To think that way, in my opinion. is prejudice. I say this because I know of some rich people who have never forgotten that they entered into this world without much, and will leave this world without much; therefore, they go out of their way to feed and help the hungry and the needy people around the world. But these few decent people are very few, and often unintentionally get lumped together with the greedy heartless rich of the society.

For some unknown reasons, most well-to-do people believe that the more they pile up their fortunes, the happier and more secure they are. Analogously speaking, if you live in a secluded spacious place, and have so much wealth, but you are surrounded by very poor and needy people all year round, how peaceful would you feel in the night, knowing that you are surrounded by starving people? Knowing that there are desperate and starving people around your neighborhood might not give you a peaceful and comfortable sleep at night. Unless you are a rich narcissist, you have to admit that when you arrived here on earth via birth, you did not have anything with you other than your naked little body with a mouth to receive nourishments from someone else (being your mother, etc.), and the day or night you exit this world, you will have no veto on what or how much of your wealth will accompany you to your grave.

Yes, I will choose our form of government, namely "democratic," over any other form of government, as long as "democracy" does not turn into a nest of cold- hearted bureaucrats who in some occasions create a "caste" system in the very heart of a democratic society. I know our democratic system is not perfect, however; there is always room to improve. Yes, "capitalism" and "communism" are at odds. Both systems need major correction, because they are not democratic. For instance, pure "capitalism" creates a concept of stratification, and as a result we have to deal with global stratification where industrialized countries position themselves in the center. These core (industrialized) countries have the most power in the world economic system, followed by second world countries like China, and eventually the countries known as "peripheral" countries, followed by the underdeveloped and young governments. The peripheral countries are known to suffer from hunger, lack of clean water, and droughts, and in many cases, they are ruled by brutal dictators. Whatever they produce from their meager farms, does not give them a right to name the price of their products in the world market; the buyer sets the price. Therefore, the lives of millions from these poor and young governments remain in the hands of the most powerful nations. I have been in the Soviet Union, and I have been in socialist countries; I witnessed what dictatorship rule did to Uganda in early 1971, and later to Zimbabwe under the rule of Robert Mugabe. I am shocked to see some Western leaders rubbing shoulders with dictators of the world. Democracy is not perfect, but it can be improved and sensitized to respond to the needs of its citizens. In a democratic system, there is "hope" of a better hour, day, or year.

There are many weaknesses in our system of government which should have been addressed hundreds of years ago. Take for instance the issue of skin color which has been one of the most agonizing and embarrassing issues in this country. However, without exonerating America, "skin color" discrimination is world-wide. Not a single continent is free from this deadly cancer. The skin color becomes the defining factor, and a barometer to tell who is intelligent, and who is not; who is guilty just by sight, and who is innocent until proven guilty. The darker your skin, the more you are a suspect of a crime until proven not guilty. So, if you are black, your innocence only applies in your kitchen or bedroom. The moment you step out, you are guilty of any crime all day until you get back in your house. You probably ask, how do I know this? I know this because I am a black man, and have had personal experiences where I wished I had a way to write a letter to my Creator, asking why my skin color is hated so much. There were times I wanted to stand on the highest mountain on earth just to ask God one simple question: "God why did you paint yourself so white? And are you only the God of the white people?" After many years of not being able to resolve this personal issue in my head, I came to the conclusion that the God I worship is colorless and genderless. The Creator of seen and unseen, cannot be trapped and defined by a creature. The God I worship cannot be caged in a building or monopolized by any race, gender, or country. The older I became and the more I travelled the world, I came to the conclusion that every woman I meet on a street is my sister and every man I meet on the street is my brother. The God I worship is beyond and above space and time. The anthropomorphism approach does not give any creature a conclusive ability or authority to criticize or question the existence of a person God created. How many of us chose our parents, or asked to be born where we call our birthplace? We are all recipients of somethings we had no control of. At times we ignore the fact that a "human being" is more than physiology. I do not believe that poverty has a color, or gender. To attach "poverty" to color of the skin or gender or race is pathetic. Racism is found in every level of society, yet we profess publicly we are not racists. In this way we find ourselves discussing racism without racists. As Eduardo Bonilla-Silva (2010) argued in detail, the persistence of racial inequality in our country shows its ugly face in three areas, namely: (a) affordable education for all our children; (b) affordable health care for all and (c) employment opportunities for all able bodies. (Bonilla-Silva, Eduardo. Racism without Racists, 2010).

CHAPTER ELEVEN:
RACISM IN THE 21ST CENTURY

I am compelled to share my thoughts with you in regard to this issue which seems to vibrate through our minds, day and night. Despite popular inclination to think otherwise, there does not exist a so-called "race gene". Rather, race exists as a product of large sociopolitical processes and historical contexts. For instance, from the advent of the slave trade and colonization to the continuous process of global integration, with post colonialism and the collapse of the Iron Curtain, national and cultural meanings of race have changed greatly. Well, is that a bad thing or a good thing? Sorry to say, "racism" is deeply embedded in much of social reality in our country. However, just because racism is ingrained into the social institution to which everyone belongs and participates, that does not mean that the system cannot change or shift gears. Discrimination involves the application of power and domination by those in possession of it, in symbolic, economic, and political ways. America has been living with this dreadful disease known as "racism and discrimination" for over three centuries, with not much to brag about. How close are we to liberation day? If, as Americans, we give up now due to lack of meaningful changes or progress, then we will surely fall into the darkest pit of humanity. Racism/discrimination is a relentless disease which can destroy souls and minds of people.

More times than I care to remember, I have been asked how I understand or decipher the slogan **BLACK LIVES MATTER**. My response has been, how do you decipher, **WHITE LIVES MATTER**? Of course, every life matters, but why are we discussing something which is obvious to any human being alive. As you think about it, what caused people of color to verbally and loudly say **BLACK LIVES MATTER**? For many years now, people of color knew and understood that their lives, or black lives, matter, despite the suppression and dismissal by the white people for centuries. Systematic suppression of people of color by white people for centuries, made people of color invisible in the eyes of white people. People of color had been treated as shadows, and their existence remained irrelevant. Their labor is essential in the areas where white people do not want to touch. In the world of economic stratification, they remain at the bottom of the ladder. For over three hundred years they helped build the economy of this country, and yet they are still at the bottom step of the economic ladder. They have been segregated for years, and live in the most depressive part of the American cities. Those who succeed to break away from poverty, are normally looked at suspiciously, as if they illegally got where they are. So, our question to the people on this planet earth should be: *"How many more years before a black person becomes a person?"* It is insanity and stupidity, to believe that a color of skin defines a person. Of course, *all* lives matter. Only the feeble-minded people would define a person by the color of the skin. Human-ness is not determined by height, gender, age, or skin color. Of course, many people of color had been conditioned and hypnotized to believe that they could never touch the glass ceiling. Imagine growing up in a society where all your life what you see and hear is that you are "garbage" and will remain that way the rest of your life. Or growing up in a society where you were not allowed to read or write, a place where you are not allowed to gather for prayers. The fear was: if you allow them to meet in groups, they may coordinate ways to free themselves or ways to rebel and start demanding to be treated like human beings. For years Black Americans were not allowed to go to school. They were just tools, or rather farm- equipment. Therefore, the slave masters were paranoid; they were afraid these slaves might figure out ways to support themselves and live like human-beings. For hundreds of years, they had been denied the right to think for themselves, and told that the best they could ever hope for was to be good and obedient slaves. That is what I call mental genocide. I have known inner city schools in this country where teachers drive from their suburban homes into inner city schools, and teach day in and day out, whether the students connect or not. At the end of the day, they drive back to their quiet and luxurious homes as the students go back to their run-down homes. To put it differently, the students go back to the reality of poverty, and the teachers go back to their heavenly blessed homes and communities. How can such a teacher nurture such students, if he/she does not have a clue of where these students are coming from? There is a great gap here, because the teachers may be talking about how great it is going to be for his/her students to succeed in college in the future, and get better jobs, while at the same time the students are wondering about a hamburger or something to eat because their stomachs are growling because they left home without any breakfast. The teachers' intentions might be good, however there is a huge gap between the teacher's intention and the students' immediate needs. Sometimes it helps when teachers remember the basic stages of Maslow's hierarchy of needs. It is a simple fact that physiological needs are the most prepotent of all. A teacher may have great ideas and advice regarding the future which awaits these students; however, if these students left their homes without any breakfast, the teacher can saturate them with great news about the future but might as well talk to the trees because the students' focus will remain on food. Those teachers who may not remember Maslow's hierarchy of needs, might falsely conclude that inner city students are either cognitively challenged or do not want to learn what will make their lives better.

According to Maslow's theory, basic needs have to be met first, such as physical needs, etc. Maslow believed that human needs are hierarchically organized, with more basic needs found toward the bottom of the hierarchy and the self-actualization needs at the top of the pyramid. He divided the hierarchy of needs into five levels. At the base of the hierarchy are the "physiological needs". These include needs that are of prime importance to the immediate survival of the individual (food, water, air, and sleep) as well as the long-term survival of the species (for instance, a need for sex). The next level up are needs for safety. These have to do with shelter and security, such as having a place to live and being free from the threat of danger. Maslow believed that building a life that was orderly, structured and predictable also fell under safety needs. For instance, having your car inspected prior to a long trip might be seen as an expression of your safety needs. The third level in Maslow's hierarchy is a need for belonging. Humans are a very social species, and most people possess a strong need to belong to a group or groups, such as families, sororities /fraternities, churches, clubs, or teams. Possibly some people find a need to belong to some groups such as gangs. Maslow felt that sometimes gangs provide group membership to people who might otherwise feel alienated or excluded from groups available to members of the dominant culture.

The fourth level of Maslow's hierarchy of needs contains esteem needs. There are really two types of esteem: (a) esteem from others, and (b) self-esteem (the latter always depending on the former). For instance, we want to be seen by others as competent, as strong, and as able to achieve. We want to be respected by others for our achievements and our abilities. We also want this respect to translate into self-esteem; we want to feel good about ourselves, to feel that we are worthwhile, valuable, and competent. The fifth level is the self-actualization need: the need to develop one's potential, to become the person one was meant to be. You might think this is difficult, as it assumes that one must first figure out who one was meant to be. However, self-actualizers seem to just know who they are and have few doubts about the direction their lives should take. However, most people are not self-actualizers. Instead, most are working hard to satisfy the lower needs, trying perhaps to acquire esteem from others to bolster their status, prestige, and egos, or trying to satisfy belongingness needs through their relationship with family members or people in other primary groups. By the way, this does not mean that one must make great contributions to become self-actualized. It is possible for ordinary as well as extraordinary people to achieve self-actualization. What

I would like you think about is the fact that we cannot ignore the primary (basic) needs of a human being because we are too busy trying to save the soul of the hungry, cold, or physically sick who have no place to sleep. The number of homeless people is growing every year. They are not only hungry, but they get sick like anyone else; and yet they cannot be treated because they do not have insurance; they cannot afford to pick up a prescription because the medicine will take all the money they have for food. How many times have you seen a person asking for help to get a cup of coffee or a piece of bread, and you turned your head away while you are waiting for the light to change so you can get to your destination in a hurry, to do what you believe to be more important in your life. One of many excuses you make is that, "well she/he can get help from the government. Look, I pay taxes, I give my money to church, I volunteer in many ways, and I do not want to feel guilty turning my head away". If you are a Christian and reading this, I would like you to check out what Jesus told his disciples, when they were so concerned about the safety of people who had been listening to Jesus for many hours. Since they came from different places and it was getting very late, the disciples appropriately suggested that they should go back home. Jesus's response was "feed them first" (Mathew 14: 16-18). In 1897, W.E.B. Du Bois said: "It is a peculiar sensation, the double-consciousness, the sense of always looking at one's self through the eyes of others.....One ever feels his twoness—An American, a Negro; two souls, two warring ideals in one dark body, whose dogged strength alone keeps it from being torn asunder." (W.E.B. Du Bois, The Souls of Black Folk, 1903). Prior to W.E.B. Du Bois, a formerly enslaved person, Olaudah Equiano (1789), referring to the practice of separating husbands and wives, parents from children, in order to meet the request of the slaves' buyers at the market, said to those who were selling him:

" O, ye nominal Christians, is it not enough that we are torn from our countries and friends to toil for your luxury and lust of gain? Why are parents to lose their children, brothers and then sisters, or husbands their wives? Surely this is a new refinement in cruelty—and adds fresh horrors even to the wretchedness of slavery." (Equiano, O. The Interesting Narrative of the Life of Olaudah Equiano, 1789). Those sharp and truthful words landed on deaf ears and rebellious hearts. Realistically, how far are we today from those voices of the past?

CHAPTER TWELVE:
POLICE OFFICERS VS. PEACE OFFICERS

The murder of George Floyd in Minneapolis by four Police Officers in 2020 angered many people around the world. However, if we stop and think about it, we soon realize that the slaughtering of people of color in this country is not new at all. The police culture is very much aware of their unlimited immunity. As a nation, we created an elite force and armed them and dispersed them with unlimited immunity. So we should not be surprised when Police Officers are eager to shoot and ask questions later. They are sent to various parts of our cities under the umbrella of policing, with permission to act as they wish. As a nation, we failed to differentiate a "police role" from that of a "soldier". City councils have failed to define the duties and limits of a Police officer. Historically, a police officer was supposed to be a "Peace Officer", a person whom citizens trusted and whose advice was valued. A police officer was supposed to be a trusted friend, whose main duty was to maintain peace. This expectation is long gone in the United States of America. Today the line between a "police officer" and an "army officer" (soldier) has faded. Currently many believe that trained soldiers would do a better job of patrolling/policing the communities and cities than police officers. Police officers have lost credibility, especially among people of color. Without exonerating police officers, the problem of bullying and discounting the legitimate rights of people of color, goes deeper than city administrations and state governments. Discounting and pushing aside the complaints of people of color in regard to police brutality is a national cancerous tumor which will eventually kill the dream of America being a democratic nation. Racial discrimination, prejudice, and blunt hatred of people of color has saturated every public and private institution in the country, and in this case, religious institutions are not exempt. Police officers do not come from a foreign country; most of them were born here, and exposed to racism, discrimination, and prejudice in their communities, often where there are no people of color except the ones on the television screen. These young people grow with an unrealistic view of people of color. In spite of all this, I personally have met some white police officers whose philosophy meets the original police educational foundation, meaning: every person is innocent until proven guilty, and not the other way around. In dictatorial regimes, a person is guilty until proven otherwise. In those governments the person with a gun and a badge has the power over the citizen's status. The judicial system is nothing but a rubber stamp. Sometimes I wonder why we dislike dictatorial regimes even though we are doing the same thing. Our judicial system is limping and about to fall apart. The police union is not only strong financially but also can have the best lawyers to defend their members. When money becomes the issue, the rights of the victim get thrown out the window, or the family of the victim is given some technical justification for what the police had done; unfortunately, many times the victims are not there to defend themselves, because they are already dead. The killer gets out of court with a symbolic pinch on the shoulder, meaning he/she will continue to wear the badge in the same city or get hired by another city's police force.

As I mentioned elsewhere, I have known some "Peace Officers" who in the midst all the confusion, kept the concept of peace as a driving force. Unfortunately, the culture they work in and the schooling they went through did not prepare them adequately to fit the concept of "Peace Officer". The education institutions failed to underline their central goal which is keeping peace in the community. The institutions failed to educate them in the area of "human behavior"; instead, these institutions focused on training rather than educating them. Unfortunately, these graduates are expected to go out into communities where there are various problems such as physical or psychological problems, or issues related to racial discrimination, prejudice, relationships, street drugs, or homelessness. Very few of these young men/women took adequate psychological courses before they took their internship assignments. All along my concern has been: how do you train and arm a young person, who might have psychological issues which remain hidden? By the way, I am not suggesting that police officers become psychologists, rather, I am pointing out that, some of these cases of police officers who react and brutally kill those he/she was supposed to protect, might be a good indication that the system is putting guns in the hands of people who should be in psychiatric offices for therapy.

What comes to mind is the case of Charles Whitman in Texas. After killing both his wife and his mother, he barricaded himself at the top of the University of Texas observation tower. When it was all over, he had shot 38 people, 14 of them dead. In the suicide note he wrote before he killed both his wife and his mother, the night he went to the observational tower, he asked for an autopsy to be done to see if there was anything visible wrong with him. Later the autopsy revealed a tumor a size of a walnut in the area of the brain known as "amygdala". From a scientific perspective, amygdala is a necessary part of our brain which functions like a motion detector, warning an individual of incoming danger. The problem is, this wonderful part of our brain can misread the incoming message and send a danger signal and mobilize a person to react impulsively without any merit. To put it simply, imagine a person who is walking in an area that historically had been known to have poisonous snakes. Even though it had been a long time since snakes like that were seen in the area, this individual walking on a wonderful paved side-walk, saw a little lizard five feet away crossing the side walk in a hurry. This person jumps up, screaming that he/she came so close to being killed by a poisonous snake. In reality that was just a small lizard crossing, but the person's faulty amygdala sounded the bell of imminent danger. Or take the case of four paranoid, plain-clothed police officers in New York, who pumped 19 bullets into the body of a 23-year-old immigrant from Guinea Africa in front of his apartment door. Early in the morning, Diallo was in front of his apartment building, with no weapon other than a key. The police thought he fit the description of a reported rapist in the area. They ordered him to stop and identify himself; he told them he lived there and that he had a key in his pocket. As he reached to show them the key, one of the officers tripped and fell, the other thought he had been shot, and without hesitation they fired 41 bullets, and 19 hit their target. Amadou Diallo died at the scene. He was unarmed. The object he took out of his pocket was his wallet to show the officers his identification. The internal investigation by the New York Police Department ruled that the officers acted reasonably under the circumstances. At the end they were ultimately acquitted. This goes to show you that the law in our judicial system is "white". My question is, what made the police react the way they did? Secondly, did the system fail to protect the innocent person? Or what about the case of George Zimmerman who shot and killed Trayvon Martin in Florida? Zimmerman shot Trayvon in the chest even though Trayvon was not armed and he was not involved in any criminal activities. However, Trayvon was not there to argue his case. So, we go back and ask ourselves what triggered such an impulsive action in Zimmerman? Did he really see a poisonous snake or a lizard? How often does a system put guns in the hands of mentally sick persons? How often do cities mandate a psychological test for all persons who interact with members of the community? How often does the police department make available psychological services, especially for those whose duties directly involve members of the communities? The bottom line should be: why is it that, many times, it is so difficult to establish trust between people of color and members of the police department?

Why is there such mistrust between a policeman and a person of color? The truth is, the many years of neglect and brutality which people of color continue to experience on a daily basis, have reinforced their gut feelings that police officers are not coming to their communities with an open mind, or to help solve some problems, but rather with a confirmation bias approach. Therefore, while white children would be glad to see police in their neighborhood, black children tend to bite their fingernails with fear, wondering what went wrong and what's going to happen. If there is crime in the area, police might not receive much help from the community, simply because there is no **trust** between these two groups. The younger generation of people of color in many cases has a tendency of turning away, or worse, running away when the police officers approach them. As children they perceived police officers not as friendly people, but rather as rough and tricky people whose intention is to punish or hurt people of color. Yet this is totally different in the case of young white children. For the white children, the presence of the police officers remains positive and an assurance of peace. From a psychological perspective, we know that children learn very early to differentiate friendly environments from hostile encounters. Thanks to technology, children learn much earlier to draw boundaries (who are the good and the bad persons) than we dare to believe. At this point I want to remind my readers that racial awareness and bias begin very early in children. In the September issue of "Perspectives on Psychological Science" (2021) there is well-detailed research by Sandra R. Waxman (Department of Psychology. Northwestern University) which elaborates how racial awareness and bias begin very early in life. Let us not forget: technology is a double -edged sword, and we cannot pretend to be blind or deaf. It is the duty of every parent/adult to help children see that no one is perfect; we are all human; there is a tug of war between good and evil.. Good or evil has nothing to do with color of the skin, or gender of the person or age of a person., There are good police officers and there are bad police officers. We are never certain, until it is over. Yet we need to understand that the worst failure, is failing to learn from failure. We need to remind ourselves that the police officers we hire to keep peace in our neighborhoods were once children like other children; they are not experts of life, for they have not finished up living; therefore, they are bound to make mistakes like any living person on this planet.

We should teach those who desire to become police officers, that they are not super-humans. The size of a police officer's brain is not that much different from the rest of the population they police. Being given a privilege and a chance to keep peace in the community does not translate or propel them into a level of heavenly angels. Let it be clear that those who desire to become police officers are to "serve," not to be "served". The very people they meet in these communities are actually their bosses, not servants. In the same breath, these communities need to support these officers and orient them, and welcome them as new members of these communities. They should give them a chance, and help them as they learn the nature and the life style of the community. Communities and the police departments ought to have days where adults of the communities introduce the new peace officers (police officers) as members of these communities, whose sole purpose in these communities is (and remains) to keep peace in the neighborhood, not fear and intimidation.

There should be an understanding that "policing" is a profession like any other profession in our government. One chooses to become a police officer just like any other career or professional choice in our system. To put it more clearly: no one is forced or drafted to go into this job. Like any other job in our system, it is a personal choice of a way to make a living. Like any other public job, one has a personal responsibility, to do what the job calls for. Take for instance if one prefers to become a physician, that individual must learn everything to be learned in that area of expertise/specialization. This partic-ular physician can be hired by a certain hospital or medical group. Even with his/her impressive credentials, this individual will be responsible for his/her malpractice insurance. The hospital is not going to be held responsible for the physician's negligence. My question is: "Why, when it comes to police officers, is the city expected to pay the damages incurred by its employees? By paying the damages, or settling law-suits (which are in some cases costly), the city is indirectly enabling her employees to act irresponsibly in these communities. Accountability is missing in regard to those police officers who end up making quick but tragic decisions in dark alleys of our cities. Pulling a trigger should be the last thing a peace officer has to consider. Those behind the desk or in nice and secure offices, should make sure the men and women being sent out to the communities, do not drag their personal frustrations, etc. to the area of patrol. They should not bring their family problems or frustrations into the job. No wonder these employees can act recklessly in their jobs, because they know very well that the city will take the short end of the stick. Sometimes these cases take a lot of money from the city budget, which is public money. If the city is perpetually in a rescue mode, those police officers who mistake people for brutes, will continue to shoot and ask questions later, which in many cases happens to be too late. There should be mandatory psychological testing every two years for all police officers who interact with members of these communities. A city should set aside a budget to help those who are having psychological issues in their lives. We need to realize that sometimes police officers have families, and it is not unusual for a person to drag a home problem all the way to the office or to work. The police officers need to know they can talk to someone confidentially, someone they can trust and respect.

I believe the institutions of higher learning ought to be aggressive and bold in introducing real courses which deal directly with equity, diversity and inclusion. In 2008, the American Association of Colleges and Universities (AAC&U) developed an Intercultural Knowledge and Competence Value Rubric (Bennett, J.M., 2008) that can actually provide relevant stakeholders with the related behavioral anchors for measuring the knowledge, skills, and attitudes needed to successfully navigate cultural contexts. Today we are well into 2023, with very little to show. The thread which has been holding Americans together (though not impressively) almost broke in 2020. What we saw and heard on January 6, 2021, was a prelude of what could happen or might happen if both private and public sectors do not abandon their "wait and see" posture. In most developed countries throughout the years, institutions of higher learning have played unique and major roles in alerting their societies on over-reaching or at times neglectfulness of their respectful government/regimes. Learning centers (colleges/universities) should not recoil and pretend dead or play deaf when their own societies are hemorrhaging in the intensive care units. America's oldest tumor (racism) is threatening the survivability of this nation. Racism is a national threat of which no American is exempt. It is time centers of higher learning stand up to be counted. We should keep in mind that without a unified society, or rather a stable institution, chances of a vibrant college/university are doubtful. I cannot think of a better place to turn to for help than the colleges and universities of this nation. These universities and colleges do have excellent opportunities to plant the seeds of equity, diversification and inclusion in a society which seems to have lost a sense of direction. In 2017, The American Psychological Association (APA) released "Multicultural Guidelines"; the guidelines call on educators to include multicultural coursework in the curriculum, and engage students in community-based training activities with diverse constituents. A syllabus for such courses should definitely allow the Professor to communicate his/her philosophy, expectations, requirements and other important information. There are a lot of ways to write and design a syllabus; however, we should not lose sight of the main goal, which is, at the end of the day, to adequately promote: Equity, Diversification, and Inclusion. No one person is going to give or design a syllabus for a multicultural course which fits every university/college; however, if universities/colleges of this nation design the syllabi with those goals (Equity, Diversity, and Inclusion) in mind, we can say we have a chance to dig ourselves out of the three hundred years of ignorance(racism) and a much greater chance of reaching equity and inclusion, and *never* segregation again. I am very much aware of the fact that universities and colleges of this nation are not going to become rich or make a lot of money by taking a lead in this war, but I am convinced that if they so choose to take a leap of faith, and engage the nation's worst enemy "racism", it will be not only a noble leap of faith, but also a patriotic move that future generations will remember with much respect.

CHAPTER THIRTEEN:
HUMAN MIGRATION— A NEW CHALLENGE

Not too long ago, a colleague asked me a question regarding refugees and human migration, which seems to be a global problem. I heard him clearly, however, I asked him to give me time to think about it. The more I thought about it, the more I took time to respond. I was looking for a short but well-thought-out answer to his question.

After weeks of thinking about human migration and the complexity of resettling millions of people who left their homelands for many reasons, I realized that I was not going to be able to give my colleague a short and clear answer. Of course, I have had a chance to dialogue with some of the people from Somali and some from Sudan. And years ago, I met and became friends with several refugees from Sarajevo. Yet I knew that such a small sample would not have given me a wider perspective of the millions of people who fled their home countries because, in spite of the deep love and emotion attached to a birth place, staying in the home country was no longer a smart or safe choice. Many of these people fled their homeland without much on their backs. For some, to flee the ancestral land was dreadful. The only choice they had was to stay in the birthplace and be butchered by merciless dictators, or take a chance and run away from there as soon as possible. It is estimated that currently there are about 79 million people who fled their homelands due to war, brutal governments, hunger and starvation, etc. Many of these people had been in refugee camps for several years without any prospect of having an opportunity to start life in a decent country. The original question from my colleague prompted me to explore a number of fields in search of "human migration," which led me into social psychology, anthropology, biology, sociology and religion. As I previously said, none of us chose to be born at a particular place and time. Refugees normally do not leave their homelands willingly; for most of them, it is a matter of "run away while you still can, or stay and end up in a grave". Grammatically, there is a slight difference between a "migrant" and a "refugee". A refugee has no choice left: either get out of the homeland or end up dead; whereas a "migrant" is looking for a better life or consciously searching for ways to use his/her talents to snap out of poverty and live a better life. Migrants leave their countries which are historically and politically stratified, countries where the few on the top dominate the wealth of the country; it is very close to a "caste-like" system. Such countries stifle the ingenuity of those who happen to be born into a lower caste. These individuals have big dreams but are not given a place and room to actualize these dreams; therefore, out of frustration, they see the only window left for them is "migration".

The act of going from place to place in search of comfort or relief is not new at all. Itinerancy is as old as life itself. If the shifting of one or more atoms from one position in a molecule to another is normal and can be understood, why is it difficult to understand human beings who rove from time to time in search of better conditions? Coming from a nomadic tribe (Maasai), I have a much better understanding of migration than many of my friends who did not grow up in that part of the world. Roving is natural, it is in all of us. Scientific discoveries do actually entertain this concept. All normal creatures move from "uncomfortableness" to better or rather a more "comfortable" position. For instance, imagine you have a "toothache" all night. I guess the next morning you might make an attempt to see a dentist. Analogously, there is a built-in desire to move away from pain to comfort or a "no-pain" position. It is my belief that medical centers are not about to shut down major medical research centers in the near future, notwithstanding major breakthroughs in successful vaccines in most industrialized countries. During the height of COVID-19, the nation's medical centers were perceived as "centers of hope" in regard to giving millions much needed relief.

Call it a curse or a blessing, there is a strong instinctual drive in all creatures to gravitate to "comfort," or in some cases "safety." As human beings we are constantly searching for physical comfort. Animals in the wild rove every year in search of green pastures and water. Millions of animals migrate between Tanzania and Kenya every year, depending on where they can find food. Rain and drought in East Africa dictate and trigger the migration of millions of wildebeest. They cross the national boundaries at will. The point I want to convey is: migration of human beings is not new, and it is not an elaborate scheme to crowd and take over another country's fortune. Think for a while, if somebody is escaping from a burning building and desperately running to your home needing help, would you shut your door, telling the worried and crying person, "go call the Fire Department, I do not have time. I am going to bed because I have to work tomorrow"? How would you feel if somebody treated you in that manner? We need to keep in mind that "living" calls for perpetual motion. A human being is not a piece of rock on the bank of a river which might have been there for thousands of years. We are fully aware that a person enters this life as a tiny helpless baby, then continues to develop and change incrementally; however, this particular baby goes through changes (developmental stages), reaches the peak of development, and slowly begins to turn to the other direction of life, with anticipation (hope) of passing a torch to a new generation. This very person moves from dependence to independence and back to dependency. My point is: we as human beings are constantly moving from one position (situation) to a new or different position. To put it differently: moving from primary to secondary is not unusual in humanity. It is absolutely natural to rove from time to time without any definite destination, in search of a better condition. For instance, during the height of Covid-19, the need to get a vaccine became a priority. I personally did not care where I went to get vaccinated. The urgency of avoiding the disease was prominent in my mind. There is a built-in desire to move from pain to comfort, or from death to life. This need to gravitate to comfort is innate; it is something a person does not plan ahead of time; rather, it is something which overcomes a person and pushes this person to seek the alternative, in this case, "comfort".

It is not an exaggeration to say the 21st Century will go down in history as the century of an unprecedented number of refugees and asylum seekers. Our dilemma is the fact that the world population is alarmingly growing much faster than any of our anticipations. Unfortunately, our planet earth is not expanding, and its resources might not be adequate or sufficient. Food and water, which are essential to human life, will continue to be insufficient, which means the world will continue to have a very difficult time sustaining billions of people. Planet earth is not and will not be able to provide for or adequately feed all of the hungry people around the world. Earth is not expanding, and yet the population numbers are going up. How do we keep a balance between world population and food products? I am afraid our world is faced with multifarious problems stemming from dictatorial rules, droughts, wars, beliefs (religions). Let us face it: mismanagement of planet earth is proving to be our greatest enemy. At the same time, the stratification system is turning out to be a major problem in the world. Lack of food and water will remain as the major triggers of the "Third World War". Destruction of human lives will be unimaginable. The underserved, the hungry population will reach a boiling point, and no threat will deter them.

The wealthy countries may not be able to eradicate all the problems of millions of people in the underdeveloped countries, or resettle them; it would be of utmost importance, however, for industrialized countries to help millions of would-be migrants to feel safer in their own countries, by doing everything possible to show dictators that their ruthless governing is barbaric and will not be rewarded. Having said that, we should keep in mind that human migration is always going to be a reality, as it has been experienced for centuries. As I am writing this, there is a possibility of many people trying to get away from barbaric killing going on in their own lands. Afghan civilians are caught in the middle of uncivilized merciless killers whose main goal is to install the worst dictatorial regime under the pretense of Islamic law (sharia). This segment of Afghans believe they are doing their country a favor by purging Afghanistan by using barbaric killing and intimidation. In their law, women are subhuman, they are owned like property. The men are paranoid, and unusually nervous and irrational. Of course, a few people might be able to escape the onslaught going on in Afghanistan, but where will they go? Many industrialized countries have closed their borders. Some countries claim that they cannot over-populate their countries anymore; secondly, they cannot afford to take care of more refugees. True, these are legitimate concerns given the fact that many of the European countries are much smaller than Afghanistan. The sad thing is, those industrialized countries which dealt with Afghanistan in previous years, now distance themselves from the ensuing bloodshed which civilians are experiencing. Of course, it was a bad policy to invade and establish a military presence in a country whose rulers use archaic laws. Let me say this, as long as Afghanistan is on fire, and as long as the world still has "terrorist groups" nesting in remote places in the world, the industrialized countries should not sleep with both eyes closed. Too many Americans have lost their lives in that country already. The question in the minds of many remains: for how long and when will the Afghans settle their internal differences? When will they ever grow up and realize that the days of babysitters are gone?

Certain Western countries lost many lives in Afghanistan by getting in the middle of "smart- manipulators" who refused to sit down and settle their differences. Super-powers should not let themselves be used in a situation like that, for it sends a signal to other brutal regimes to stir up some trouble with a hope that Americans would be readily available to get in the middle of home grown and rather manipulative family disagreements. Industrialized countries should find ways to dry the wells of terrorism around the world without being stuck in the place forever. Let us remember we are still in

South Korea, as a buffer against North Korea. The question many would like to know is this: does the international community reimburse America for policing the world? How many years will it take before people realize that there are other ways to persuade these nations to settle their differences without killing each other? Besides American military power, the other option would be financial muscle which can be used to persuade these hungry and greedy dictatorial governments to settle their disputes without outside help. Certainly no one is safe until we are all safe; however, the global peace should be a responsibility of every independent nation in the world. America has to keep an eye on these trouble spots of the world, but should not intervene unless the dictators are ruthless and ignoring human rights as enumerated in the United Nations charter. Yet in the same breath, let the industrialized countries encourage regimes to take care of their citizens not by intimidation and threats but by rule of law. Dictators should not be rewarded by the industrialized countries; they should know they are not safe or secure until and unless their respective citizens are secured. Also let us remember there are other means and ways to dry the pool so this bad mosquito does not lay eggs. Let me be clear, notwithstanding, the act of going from place to place in search of comfort or relief is not new at all.

In regard to human migration, I noticed that some years back when ISIS was very active, it recruited followers from many parts of the world, particularly from European countries which generously took in refugees from war-torn countries. Those acts of kindness by the host countries are to be highly commended. The truth is, individually most European countries are small, but they were willing to resettle those refugees, whereas larger industrialized countries for some reasons are overly hesitant and restrictive. One thing I observed and monitored very carefully was how the younger generation, which accompanied their parents during the relocation to those generous countries, behaved and reacted. I noticed there was a "disconnect." Parents who escaped death in their homelands, were openly thankful to their host countries or communities. A few years later, ISIS began to recruit followers from the children of these families which had resettled in European countries. I was shocked to see that younger persons from these newly resettled families were willing to go back to ISIS and join the ranks. It was then that I realized that, what was becoming obvious, was the fact that these refugees spent too much time (symbolically) as guests. Yes, they were welcomed as guests, but were not feeling that these were going to be their permanent homes or new home countries. They were lacking the authentic feeling of belongingness. Deep down they had a feeling that they will never be able to go back to the old countries, but at the same time they did not develop that feeling of belongingness, or terminate the fantasy of "birth place". Within the thought of being a "guest" there is a hidden question in the mind of a guest, which keeps saying, for how long? Practically, there is a limit of being a guest; at a certain point a guest needs to start helping around the house, and learn a few things to make the stay more homey, and have a feeling of contribution. It was even worse for their teenagers who left their homelands in a big hurry and confusion. They left their familiar locations, friends, and childhood dreams behind. To wipe off those dreams and images in their minds, proved to be very difficult. For most of these young people, they believed going back and fighting to restore what was theirs was the only right thing to do. These strange and unrealistic dreams in the minds of these young refugees shocked the parents as well as the host communities.

ISIS used attractive propaganda to lure these young people back to their ruined countries with a promise that whatever dreams and expectations they lost during the conflict could be realized. Through that propaganda and deceit, these young people who accompanied their parents as they ran away from a destructive war, now heard a new voice which promised to restore their childhood dreams. Using that tactic, ISIS managed to drive a wedge between these young people and their parents. Both parents of these teenagers and the host communities were shocked. Yes, the parents were both shocked and embarrassed to realize that their own children were willing to join the same groups which had destroyed their ancestral lands. It was painful for those parents to watch the ISIS propaganda parading these young people as liberators and soldiers fighting for a good cause. I do not think the parents did anything wrong, nor do I think host countries knowingly did anything wrong. In my opinion, the guest status was not built on a principle of weaning "guest-status" to gradual "ownership or partnership" concept. Guest-status can get stuck and fail to reach a "partnership" level. Metaphorically speaking, these young people who went back to ISIS (known for their brutality) had physically accompanied their parents to these new lands and cultures, but they left their heads (thoughts) and hearts in the old countries. Emotionally, they never left their birth places. Well, the situation could have been different had both the guest and the host cleared up a few things right from the beginning, namely: (a) from now on this country is your country, love it, serve it with dignity; (b) the new country will not try to strip or ignore your old culture; however you (guest) have to make an effort to accommodate (gradually) the host's culture just as much as the host will accommodate the culture of the guest. Both the host and the guest will make an effort to learn from each other. To put it differently, the host will never be able to replace or duplicate what the guest lost, but can reduce the pain of the guest by being patient and understanding while helping the guest to find new meanings, new friends, and a new purpose to live. I also think the host can gently help the guest understand that life has no guarantee of anything; in life changes are inevitable, and wherever you find yourself, that is your home. My point is, there are two terms in sociology: assimilation and acculturation. In regard to refugees, there should never be an effort to introduce "assimilation." Assimilation is the attempt to strip a person of language, custom, culture, religion and beliefs. To do that to a refugee or immigrant, is like recreating that person; whereas "acculturation" is the willingness to learn something from this new person and have the new person learn something from you. In acculturation you do not strip a person of his/her culture in order for you to accept him/her. In acculturation both the host and the guest exchange ideas as equals. A person under acculturation feels worthy and ready and willing to move from "guest" to "friend". It was easy for ISIS to recruit those young persons because they did not feel a sense of belonging in the host countries. I hope both the host countries, and the refugees learn to invest in their relationships, shorten the period of being a guest, and let the relationship be based on acculturation.

CHAPTER FOURTEEN:
PEACE

The term "peace" cannot survive in isolation. Alone it remains meaningless. By this I mean, "peace" must remain relational to be meaningful and understandable. One has to ask whether the situation is "peaceable" (shaket/shketah in Hebrew). At this point the basic question here is whether our world is "peaceable." By "peace" do we mean there is only one side or one meaning of "peace" (thought or feeling, etc)?

Ultimately, is "peace" free of contradictions; free of the coincidence of opposites? In the Kiswahili language (mainly spoken in East African countries) "peace" is known as "amani," yet "amani" does not eradicate all the inconveniences of life. There is, however, a hidden expectation in "amani;" that is, that in spite of all the wrinkles of life, there remains a clear expectation that under "amani," life remains manageable and sustainable. The dream of pure eradication of ups and downs of life is not attainable; however, that does not deter a person from wishing another person "peace" (amani).

For those of us who are Christians, what did Christ mean when he appeared to his disciples, and instead of asking how they were doing, the first word to them was "**peace**"? Did Christ mean their troubles such as sickness and death were over? Did they not continue to live and later died and were buried like other people of their time? Therefore, critics would ask, "what difference did that proclamation of "peace" from Christ amount to?" Well, from my perspective, that pronouncement of "Peace" from Christ gave them a new outlook on life, a new perspective of life. From there on, they realized they will also be victorious at the end. For them, the word "peace" picked up a different meaning: it was no longer just a word, but rather a gentle, powerful assurance that He was alive, and they were to stop worrying. Prior to Christ's appearance, the disciples were scared, and that was the reason they had locked themselves in. They feared for their lives and did not know what the mob was going to do to them. You can imagine a group of people shoulder to shoulder in a locked building, afraid to step outside, and all of a sudden, their master and leader who was supposedly killed, appears in their midst, and the first word was "Peace," in a language and voice with which they were very much familiar. Instant reaction could have been probably screaming, or covering their faces, wondering whether they were imagining the whole thing; nevertheless, they realized it was not imagination, it was their Jesus Christ, their leader who was killed and buried. Prior to this incident, their future had looked gloomy and disastrous, but now, by and through His appearance, their doubts and fears were replaced by assurance that their Lord was alive, and death had lost its sting. Fear and nervousness had no more power over them. Therefore, the triangle was complete, namely: Faith---Hope---Peace. Of course, they continued to do all the essentials in life, but now with greater hope of the new life. They were not freed from ordinary human needs, however this time they became aware that they were going through this life towards the promised place. The promises of Christ to them became clear, and "doubt" was lost. The fear of physical harm lost its sting. Symbolically, after the appearance of Christ in their midst, their heart beats and blood pressure became normal. Time became precious for them; they had no time to waste. That spoken word, "Peace be with you," asserted and strengthened their faith; it pushed them to become good stewards of life's talents.

In my mind the word "**peace**" is relational, it cannot be understood fully in isolation. Imagine a triangle or, if you can, draw one on a piece of paper. On one side of the triangle write **Hope**, on the second side write **Faith**, and on the third side of the triangle write **Peace**. These are the major pillars of religion. They work in concert. They are eternally linked. What is "faith"? Some will say it is a belief in something, or believing in God or something significant in your life. Without theologizing this term, let us just say, it is a surrendering of yourself to, or pouring yourself on the "ultimate Other". Then **faith** rubs shoulders with trust, something you totally rely on, something you have no doubt about, and no words to describe it. It is a total surrender to a "being" or "God". Your entire life is in the hands of this "being" (could be "God" or something else). **Hope** is a state of relentless "expectation" of the fulfilment of the awaited promise. Hope rides over all hills of despair and celebrates the yet to come peace. The last part of our triangle is **peace**. Now this stage is the pinnacle and the final stage of the journey of faith.

My definition of "peace" as a lad has evolved tremendously. I no longer think of "peace" as something or condition of tranquility which can be achieved by just a magical wish. I am now able to think and view "peace" not as the absence of opposites, but rather a meeting of two realities harmoniously. In peace, differences are not conflictual but rather complementary. The term "peace" is not the absence of disagreements in any relationship, but it is the ability to admit that neither side alone has the ultimate truth or solution to our human predicament.

Normally, where there are two entities (persons, ideas), there we find different opinions. For instance, in marriage counseling, normally a counselor encourages couples to acknowledge their differences, and treat them not as a threat but rather as a challenge which should serve as a source of ongoing dialog in a marriage. In general, parties need to maximize their common and basic principles or things they have in common, and minimize their differences. Minimization in this context does not mean the eradication of the opposite traits, but rather that individual differences must let go of personal and dear traits for the sake of attaining the union. In principle, a good relationship is one in which a person is not only a receiver, but equally a giver and a receiver. A failure to accept our human nature, which is a composition of weakness and strength, intelligence and ignorance, holiness and evilness, seems to be one of our biggest problems. Until we lift our souls to the Creator and source of our "being-ness", humanity will continue on the path of self-destruction. We are our worst enemies; the hate of others, and demonization of those who do not pray the way we do or have different interests in life that we are not familiar with, makes one wonder how many heavens are there, and what color is God? Does God speak some African languages, or He only speaks European languages? Does God care about the "homeless"? Is God only in the mind of the believer, or is God above our theologies and political squabbles and ideologies? What are the answers to these basic but important questions? I assume you have answers, and are probably content, or else you are just like some of us who are still searching for the answers.

The term "peace" is not divorced from a cultural communication. This word (peace) cannot be understood outside or apart from the speaker. I mean there are as many meanings of "peace" as there are cultures and languages. Customs and languages do ultimately shape the meaning of the term "peace". It should be obvious that "peace" is not a state which can be imposed on someone or somebody. It cannot be forced on somebody, and it cannot endure if it is generated by force. The tranquility of it is encapsulated in trust. Mistrust destroys human relationships, and on a larger scale generates wars in the world. A nation or a country which is so low in trust, ends up becoming its own worst enemy. Classic examples are the way that world super powers communicate in regard to international affairs. Some governments spend billions of their currency each year spying on not only foreign governments but also their own citizens. Every power wants to have an upper hand, and as a result, international meetings where heads of state meet to tackle natural disasters, turn into a place of flexing muscles. Nations are suspicious of each other, and therefore they intoxicate themselves with lies, for no one wants to tell the truth for fear of being vulnerable. See what went on in the WWII meetings between the Germans and the British, or meetings between Russians and Hitler, etc. At all those meetings, no one was courageous enough to tell the truth. As a result, millions lost their lives.

Chapter Fourteen: Peace

It takes much courage to forge "peace", and I do not see that happening in the near future. As mentioned elsewhere, analogously speaking: life is simultaneously sweet and bitter, nurturing and destructive. To be human could be the trickiest reality, that neither angels in heaven nor demons in hell have personal knowledge of. Being human is being able to balance the opposing realities simultaneously. Differences between nations, people and beliefs are real; however, our humanity holds us all together, for we share the essentials of life irrespectively. Let us be honest: I know and you know that "discrimination" and "racism" are fueling hate between young and old; between women and men; between West and East nations; between black and white; between rich and poor; between ghettos and suburbs; between major religions and less known religions; between industrialized nations and poor nations; between the healthy and the sick. Until each of us admits our failure, until you and I confess and tell the truth that no person is free until everyone is free, no person can attain peace until we are all in it together. Peace is not tangible; it is above and beyond human ingenuity; it is a combination of being able to speak the truth, and a feeling of surrendering your entire being to the One who is the source of life. So let us ask ourselves, do we have peace in America, and is it achievable? Those around and close to us---are they enemies, or fellow citizens who happen to have a desire and need to live just like everyone else, so we do not have to worry about their intention? Or is it true that hate and violence have grown exceptionally, to a point where most people's blood pressure and heart rates are dangerously alarming?

It has been very difficult to comprehend the term "peace" in light of the instability and barbaric killing going on in the world. Unfortunately, for the last few years, hate and discrimination and violence have gained hurricane strength. You are probably old enough to remember a person known as Bin Laden. Without going into details, Bin Laden was a vicious and cowardly man who, on 9/11/2001, instructed his followers to attack the very heart of American democracy, inflicting heavy casualties in New York and daring to leave his mark in D.C. itself (the seat of American government). America was angry and embarrassed, that security failed to foil this dirty plot. That instance generated bitter and angry feelings in the country. Many Americans began to view Arabs or Moslems as potential terrorists. A sense of calmness and peace went through the window. Of course, such an incident created a sense of suspiciousness in many parts of the country. The name Bin Laden became synonymous with "evil". His evil actions left a permanent scar in the heart of a democratic government. It was not until President Obama's administration, that our nation got a sense of relief when Americans heard that Bin Laden was killed in his hiding place in Pakistan. Ever since the 9/11 attacks, America became more cautious about foreigners. Many changes in the law regarding foreigners were implemented, and it never occured to the legislators that, America's worst enemy might not be outside the gate, but rather at a dinner table with us all.

I previously hinted that "peace" is one of the commodities (among others) that the majority of human beings search and pray for. Our social attitudes towards those outside our inner circles might change from time to time, depending on how we understand the world around us. When things happen to us, we have a tendency of wanting to know what and why. For example, when the terrorists attacked us that morning of September 11th, we were not only shocked and angry, but we were left with the question: "**Why??**". America as a democratic country was exceedingly upset and confused. America did not deserve such a barbaric act. Some of us screamed loudly, "Why do bad things happen to good people?" Unfortunately, no one was able to give a convincing answer. To this day, I have not seen the justification for that barbaric attack. Until that time, it seemed that barbaric acts like that might happen in unstable or violent countries around the world, but not in such a generous and decent country as ours. Most of us had forgotten that America as a super power is not a sealed box of peace and prosperity. America is still one country out of many other countries in this world. I personally was reminded that no nation on earth is absolutely safe until all nations are safe. We are reminded that even the most powerful nation in the world must remain alert all the time, for the evil spirit remains hard at work.

Evil, and evil actors, come not only from without, as on 9/11, but also from within. As human beings, we have a tendency of blaming "there," and not "here." The Maasai (my tribe) say that in any bad incident, before you pass judgement or point a finger at the other person, please count how many fingers in your own hand are pointing towards yourself. What comes to mind is the horrific insurrection at the Capitol on January 6, 2021. It is shocking to think that those people who are sworn to protect the seat of democracy would turn around and become traitors and modern-day Bin Laden remnants in the heart of American democracy. I am having a hard time justifying the logic of those who are under the protection of this government plotting and actually attacking the seat and symbol of our democracy. These attackers were not sent by Bin Laden, but the recent attackers were sent by someone else from the inside. Unfortunately, that person morally and mentally proved to be unable to tell the difference between a lie and the truth. His condition seems to be beyond help, so we pray that God intervenes and shows him the light so he can be courageous enough to ask for forgiveness. That person had a mother and a father like anyone of us. Theologically God was not surprised. I believe God's foreknowledge is indisputable, so this awful act did not surprise Him. However, God also gave this principal actor, a way and opportunity to get on his knees and repent, for there is no sin so big that God cannot forgive. I personally believe that all those who were involved in the attack on American's house of liberty (January 6, 2021), are not beyond forgiveness. Denials and arguments will not establish the spirit of reconciliation and forgiveness. A crime was committed, and sincere repentance is in order. Unfortunately, this betrayer of American democracy believed he was above human laws and regulations. Failure to tell his followers the truth caused the death of a decent American. This is not time to party; rather, it is a time to stand up to be counted, to establish justice, ensure domestic tranquility, and oppose any sort of terrorism; a time to promote general welfare for all, not just a few; **it**

is also a time to end centuries of hate and slavery in America and lead the world boldly on the road to eradication of slavery and suppression of women. Adolf Hitler, the butcher of human beings, died years ago. Let us not revive him or idolize him, for doing so would be the most revulsive and abhorrent mistake in human history. Moreover, let us be honest: just because America does not have buildings or markets where slaves are being sold as animals, does not mean that people of color are now viewed by European Americans as equal partners in building and defending this nation.

For centuries African Americans have been demonized and devalued, and now it seems there is a hidden fear in the hearts of the oppressors that, if given a chance to breathe and see the light of the day, the oppressed might: (a) retaliate by demanding equal share in governing the country their ancestors helped to build; or (b) demand financial retribution. So far, those fears and speculation were never realized. The year 2009, when an African American took office as President of this country, many kept their fingers crossed, many cheered, many kept an attitude of wait and see, and some were infuriated and swore never to acknowledge the fact that America allowed a black man to be commander in-chief. Some ignorant, nervous individuals manufactured a theory that President Obama was not an American and was not born in this country, therefore he could not qualify to be a president of United States of America. All fears and speculations were just that, because President Obama, who inherited a financial mess, finished up his two terms as President and left the country financially stable and with no scandals having occurred in the White House during his administration. The world leaders liked and respected him as an equal partner. Millions of Americans who had been forgotten, were able to have a health care program.

You would think that President Obama's accomplishments would be enough to assure people that African Americans are not looking for ways to exact revenge or punish European Americans for oppressing them for centuries. Somehow, however, his success infuriated hard core racists and money-mongers who at the end organized and succeeded to have a person of their own liking in the White House. Unfortunately, that was a very bad choice for the country. Not only did that President humiliate America on the world stage, but he also mismanaged the government resources in a lot of ways. He ended his Presidency in the worst way possible. As mentioned elsewhere he (President Trump) encouraged his supporters to attack and crush the American seat of government, "the Capitol," as previously mentioned. The fact that he knew of the plot, and did not call it off, makes him equally guilty of the crime. He had a fair knowledge of the plot, and instead of calling it off, he encouraged it through his tweets. January 6, 2021, will stand as one of the darkest days in American history. Lies beget lies; however, a simple truth could have restored the dignity of the person in question. What is done is done and irretrievable, and we all know that. The right and dignified thing to do would be to tell the truth and admit he was wrong and ask for forgiveness from the people he humiliated and hurt.

My tribe has a saying: "a lie will never find you peace but rather enslave you the rest of your life." For those of us who are Christians, we are encouraged to speak and tell the truth regardless. Truth, and peace, will never become a reality as long as we fill our pockets with lies. It is time we let go of our personal pride and take the first step to ask for forgiveness, so we do not go through our lives dragging old conflicts and current garbage. We should not feel embarrassed or ashamed when we ask for forgiveness from those we have offended. Peace is good for your soul and body. From a psychological perspective, I know that behind any action or behavior there is a history as mentioned elsewhere. That is not meant to give us excuses for our present behavior (good or bad) but rather the affirmation that life is a long and complicated journey and one is continuously a student till the disembarkation.

As parents we wonder about peace when it comes to our little ones. We do not want them to be exposed to violence; we get concerned about their peace in general. Unfortunately, violence is everywhere, so how do we help our children survive in the world where it seems like everybody is working hard to maintain peace, and yet insecurity is pushing on? It is not easy to acquire "peace," especially when it is needed most. That acceptability of removing yourself from the center of a well-deserved glory, so your partner/spouse/sibling/neighbor or opponent will not walk away as a total loser, harbors the concept of peace. What I am saying is this: the definition of peace is that condition where both sides are winners and losers. For example, imagine taking an American quarter (coin), and showing it to two Tanzanian little boys whose English is still developing. Take the American quarter and show Daniel one side of the American quarter which has an eagle; and go to John and show him the same quarter, but only the side which has the human face. Now these two boys had never seen American money before. If after a while you ask Daniel to describe the American "quarter" he will definitely point out that an American quarter has an eagle; but if you ask John, he will say it has a human face. Here both boys are talking about one quarter, and each claim to have the right answer. Briefly, they are both right and wrong. John did not see the other side because he could not see both sides at the same time; so also, Daniel was also both right and wrong because he was only able to see from his side. Since we are talking about one quarter, they were both right and wrong, because they were not describing two quarters but one. Therefore, when you discuss an issue, just remember you cannot see both sides at the same time. God is the only one who can see both sides simultaneously. You might be right about a certain situation, but you only have half the truth.

Wars and conflicts begin because man makes a great attempt to be able to see both sides of the coin simultaneously. This gross mistake is repeated so often by leaders, even religious leaders, who present themselves as if they just came down from heaven with a fresh message from God, and talk about God as if they are granted a special power to know what God is thinking or planning. Sometimes it sounds like mankind wants to capture God for sale, or destroy those who do not see our way. What you and I need is to surrender to God, and pray **"Thy will be done."** People are not always going to agree most of the time; however, we need to realize that no two people are exactly the same, which I see as a good thing. Differences in thoughts and beliefs do make living exciting. Peace is the ability to realize that while there is an awareness of disunity in each person, there is also a desire for unity of the "within" in each of us. There has to be a harmonious synthesis between the subject and the object. The bottom line is: duality is not a luxury, but a pre-requisite of growth. In the last stage of the process of development, duality and opposition are harmonized and integrated into a higher synthesis.

My point is this: sincere and practical disagreements often produce realistic and strong relationships. However, I do not subscribe to the belief that there is a strong correlation between "disagreement" and "argument". Just because a couple disagrees in certain things, the disagreement does not necessitate arguments, which, by the way, harbor irrationality and tend to cloud the facts. As humans we certainly learn a lot by and through disagreements, but hardly any important thing from arguments. Normally, disagreements force people to look for alternatives or better ways to reach a goal. In other words, disagreements among family members are good because family members might be forced to re-evaluate certain rules or dogma, whereas arguments might lead to the break-up of a family. My sense is that Americans do have fundamental disagreements in areas of civil liberties, health care, voting rights, education, and jobs. Despite those disagreements, Americans have enough sense not to set fire on their own house. This was evident during the Civil Rights Movement. I stepped on American soil in the Sixties, and I did not see how this country was going to hold on together. To my surprise it held together and never let outside foes set it ablaze.

African Americans were tired of being told to wait for their freedom. They were tired of being treated as animals, robbed of their dignity. For hundreds of years, they heard the sermon of tolerance; they heard promises from those who rob them of their human dignity. They were told justice is on the way, a day of liberation is very near. Religion was used to hypnotize them and put them in a trance-like situation. For hundreds of years, they patiently waited for the day when they would achieve "humanity". Their masters made sure they remained in the dark. The law of the land was written by the European

Americans for the European Americans, and disregarded African Americans. For hundreds of years, African Americans were used to build this country, including cities, roads, and farming, all without a chance to share the fruit of their labor. If there is heaven, to which heaven did the departed African Americans go? Is God white, too? Who created people of color? If people of color are worthless, why did God create them? Christian churches used the Bible (Colossians 3:18-23) to justify slavery and suppression of women: "Wives, be subject to your husbands, as it is fitting in the Lord. Husbands, love your wives and never treat them harshly. Children, obey your parents in everything, for this is your acceptable duty in the Lord. Fathers, do not provoke your children, or they may lose heart. Slaves, obey your earthly masters in everything, not only while being watched and in order to please them, but wholeheartedly, fearing the Lord. Whatever your task, put yourselves into it, as done for the Lord and not for your masters" (New Revised Standard Version, Holy Bible, XL Edition. *Colossians 3:18-23*. 1989, p. 1086). Some thought and hoped that after all these years of waiting for the European Americans to acknowledge African Americans' contributions in nation building, the European Americans who controlled the system, should have enough sense to correct the many wrongs which had been done to African Americans for many years. Now they realized no one was going to hand them their God given dignity and freedom peacefully. They decided to join hands and go after their rights peacefully, only to be met by angry mobs. There were those who were convinced that the only sure way to gain their independence was by force. Fortunately, Rev. Dr. Martin Luther King, Jr. devised a less violent way, which would lead African Americans out of social/mental/physical oppression non-violently. That was a wise thought; however, not everybody wanted to grant the oppressor more time of trickling down equality. The oppressor's time had expired over a hundred years ago. Most of the younger generation of African Americans concluded that the oppressive regime would never remove the slavery chains off the ankles of African Americans peacefully. That being the case, they decided to take to the streets, and show the whole world the dark side of America. They were willing to shed their blood for the freedom they have been waiting for, a freedom which kept moving away every year. They wanted to know (without any more delay) whether European Americans were going to honor the constitution or not. This group of African Americans was not oblivious of the ruthlessness and brutality of law enforcement, especially in the southern states, yet they wanted their freedom so badly and were willing to die for it. Dr. Martin Luther King Jr. had the same goal, which was to force the white government to free the African Americans, remove a yoke of slavery off their tired and sore necks, and grant full equality. The only difference here was, Dr. King wanted freedom without violence; he believed "peace" would be victorious in the end. He was convinced that a peaceful approach was going to overcome the oppressor at a certain point. As a result, the white government's cruelty was exposed for the whole world to see, and the white government had to make some major changes, such as from an "exclusive" to an "inclusive" approach.

Here we see the power of love and a "non-violence" approach disarming the oppressive system. This is not to say that the movement went without some bruises, because that would be disingenuous on my part; we know some lives were lost in the process. Yet I can say confidently, "peace" exceeded violence. The world we live in remains tumultuous, thus we dare not take our eyes off the pillars of democracy, for we are not free until planet earth is free. The western nations are not free until the bells of "peace and freedom" also ring in the East, North and South of planet earth. Peace is expensive, but vital the world over. Let every soul celebrate diversity within unity.

EPILOGUE

Dear reader, my sincere appreciation for coming along this far with me. One issue I would like to mention as our conversation comes to an end is: **Equality and Opportunity are Twins.** The truth is, equality of opportunity plays an important part in the search for distributive justice, the allocation of the benefits and burdens of economic activity. Therefore, our question should be, "under what conditions is the distribution of liberties, opportunities, and goods (that society makes available to persons), just or morally fair? The distribution is just and fair if it satisfies the norm of equality of opportunity. This requires that unchosen inequalities (matters imposed on an individual in way that he/she could not have influenced or controlled) be eliminated. On the other hand, inequalities that arise from choices made by individuals who are given equal conditions initially, and a fair framework for interaction, should not be eliminated or reduced. By the way, this is the concept of a "level playing field". We need to understand that justice requires leveling the playing field by making everyone's opportunities equal and then letting individual choices and their effects dictate further outcomes. The ideal is a society in which people do not suffer disadvantage from discrimination on grounds such as race, ethnicity, religion, gender, and sexual orientation. One can understand this ideal as morally right in and of itself. One can also understand that excluding persons, for instance women, from the labor force makes markets function less efficiently and can result in the loss of valuable talents socially and economically.

The key here is the equality of opportunity. It is utterly unreasonable to expect an individual with limited opportunity to improve or make progress to the same degree as those with a high level of opportunity. In 2009 there was research done by Richard Wilkinson and Kate Pickett; they found that greater equality makes societies stronger. Generally, the findings of that research suggested that poor health and violence are more common in more unequal societies. However, when they studied social problems internationally, they found that some of these (social problems) were also more common in unequal societies. The list included: level of trust, mental illness (including drug and alcohol addiction); life expectancy and infant mortality, obesity, children's educational performance, teenage births; homicides, imprisonment rates, and social mobility. For instance, inequality is normally associated with lower life expectancy, higher rate of infant mortality, poor self-reported health, low birth-weights, AIDS, and depression. Social mobility is lower in more unequal countries. Homicides are more common in unequal societies. Having said all that, I think there are four perspectives which could lead us into more meaningful discussion: (a) It is fair to say that many problems faced by people in our society are largely caused by the institutional structure of society and not by people's own inadequacies or actions; (b) Even given societal structure's impact on individuals, people ultimately are responsible for their own actions and behavior, if not for their fate. There is free will within the boundaries of the opportunities available, boundaries that are defined by both objective and subjective realities; (c) social policies and programs can have a profoundly positive influence on society; and (d) private troubles and public issues are interrelated. I mean that private problems are embedded in public issues, and public issues are often embedded in private troubles. All four perspectives are very important because of the circumstances in which people are born and raised. Of course, there are different obstacles and opportunities confronting each individual. There are unequal capacities among people, and there are oppressive social forces. No one denies these factors as part of the reality that confronts each individual in relation to his/her own responsibility. Besides, people are sometimes so incapacitated, that their impairment makes it impossible for them to control their own actions;

therefore, they do not have a full measure of responsibility. These exceptions and external forces create a dilemma for human beings, but it seems to most of us, we must hold people responsible for their actions precisely because such a claim upon them maintains their very humanity and dignity.

The bottom line is: to what extent are people really human without assuming responsibility for their actions? Adam and Eve attempted unsuccessfully to shake off their accountability. This is to say, if one is human, one is deserving of faith in ultimate worth, in capacity to grow. Being a human being implies being responsible for one's actions in spite of adversity. There is a patronizing element in portraying vandals as social revolutionaries, and there is racism in suggesting that any group cannot be expected to live up to standards for responsible behavior. Most of us believe that poverty and other social problems derive largely from the institutional arrangements of the society in which we live. The arrangements result from an interplay between philosophical beliefs, and the demands of our society. These factors are structural in the society and simply the byplay of individuals with equal opportunity making their demands felt in a free market economy. From the tax structure, which is much less progressive (the very rich pay very little tax) than in previous decades, to the availability of social services and supports, to the punishments meted out by the penal system, I nervously observe vast inequalities in how people are treated by society. Believe it or not, there is a kind of "welfare" for the wealthy and for large industries that is not available to the poor. For some of us, solutions to social problems must be sought mainly in institutional and structural arrangements rather than in the rehabilitation of vast numbers of sick, disturbed, or uncultured individuals. Although most of us believe individuals need and deserve individualized services, the greatest help will come to most people through institutional changes such as quality education, job creation, improved housing, and equitable health services. The rhetorical argument that government is the enemy of social progress is impractical because that argument is ignoring the impact of societal structure. To entertain the belief that government programs can only make problems worse is simplistic and baseless. Sure, the voluntary efforts of people in local communities can really make a difference, and that should not be ignored. However, students of history know that major and massive social problems through the history of this country have been dealt with only through major governmental efforts including the application of fiscal resources. From the Social Security system, to Medicare, to any number of significant programs (assistance in natural disasters from coast to coast, for example), the badly needed relief came through major public efforts, most often national and not local.

Today we live in a highly complex, postindustrial society in which we all are very interdependent. We may not like it; nevertheless, as self-reliant, autonomous, and independent super people we believe ourselves to be, it might be extremely painful to admit that we are in fact integrally dependent on others, as they are on us. Let us get it straight: not all of us can repair automobiles, build bridges and roads, grow crops, or teach ourselves complex subjects; we are deeply dependent on others who are able to do those skills; at the same time, many others are dependent on our own specialized skills and knowledge. Analogously speaking, nations of the world are interdependent and function in concert. The function of your eyes is certainly different from that of your legs or your feet, but you need all of those parts to be a whole person. Each part of your body functions differently, and for you to be healthy, there has to be interdependence of the entire body. Fear and greed tend to drive us to believe that small is better than bigger, or bigger is better than that tiny particle, without which the larger picture is not complete and is lacking in totality. You cannot ignore the importance of your feet just because you have a good head or a good-looking face; each part of your body is essential for your wellness, and each part is required to function accordingly. The point is, accountability goes both ways. The government structure must be held accountable, just as much as each person in this country is held accountable.

For a number of years, I have heard conflicting theories regarding how to solve and shrink the problem of "homelessness" in this country. Yes, we are the richest country in the world, yet our cities are very much familiar with "homelessness". Almost every state and every major city has "homeless" Americans. For instance, in Washington D.C., homeless people spend nights along the street which leads to the seat of American government. The law-makers tend to play mute when the issues regarding homelessness in America are brought up. I know it is a sensitive subject; however, we need to solve it; and I would argue that the government cannot solve this problem until the homeless representatives are at the table during the discussion. In other words, we cannot find a practical solution to this problem until the day we dare to hold these victims accountable, just as we hold the government structure accountable. I strongly believe that any program which does not include or involve the very people we are trying to help, will not work or survive. We cannot create a solution behind closed doors and then bring it out for implementation. A solution to homelessness, or any other problem, must be tailored to fit the very people we intend to help. We can only do that by making them part of the planners. No amount of money, compassion, education or trick will yield lasting and favorable results without the full participation of those intended to be helped. Let me be very clear: to continue to give someone a fish, without telling the person where you got the fish, and how you caught the fish, is nothing but enslaving that person.

Homeless people do not need the "self-righteous sermons" which we tend to use to portray them as sinful and corrupt (they know themselves better than anyone else). I am not dismissing the problems caused by "stratification" in our society; what I would like to focus on is the reality of the world we find ourselves in. It is tempting to dwell in our old beliefs and theories which perceive those persons with problems such as loss of employment; human disasters such as Covid-19; or widespread disasters which affect people across the board, as: lazy, and not smart enough to pull themselves out of their problems. Some of us know people who were doing very well until the companies they had worked for, sometimes for decades, moved out of the country. Within months, these people lost their homes and joined the ranks of the homeless. Some suggested they should look for new jobs, yet these critics are forgetting one major thing: many of these people did not receive the training and the skills which the younger generation today take for granted. Going to class with your grandchildren or people who are a lot younger, whose brains are still at the peak, is not an easy thing to do. Let us keep one thing straight, and that is: poor people in this country were once working class; they were persons, and today they are still persons with little to show. There is anger and resentment plus shame found among the poor homeless people. People say, "Why do they spend the little money they have to buy drugs?" Let us not forget that in many cases drugs become a cover or blanket to conceal the true feelings of being actually homeless, without a place you can call your own. Life becomes meaningless, and hope is nowhere to be found. Individuals in our communities and states have to demonstrate how beaten down they are before our community or government intervenes. If we do not spend money and time now to slow down the growth of homelessness, we will spend more money in the future just to keep these groups barely surviving. I cannot emphasize enough, that any plan or project geared to help the homeless must make utmost effort to involve or consult the homeless people themselves. They must be part of the solution, or at least can help the government or charity organizations make meaningful and practical decisions. It should not be unusual for the government or charity organization to recruit some of the homeless population to offer their practical advice in regard to getting many of these people out of the streets. Let us not think that, just because they ended up roving from place to place in search of food or shelter, they are not perceptive and articulate. We tend to judge them just by sight. We quickly categorize them without a single word of "hello". We try to avoid them as if they are already dead. Just because they lost their homes and their jobs due to companies moving out of the country, or due to new technology which seems to replace human beings in the job market, it does not give people a right to dismiss them or judge them as rejects and blood suckers in our society.

In every sunset, there lies the sunrise. For every tear of sadness, there is a tear of happiness. Within the very heart of disappointment there lies the seed of hope; for every defeat there lies success; for every growth, there lies decline; for every giving there lies receiving; for every discouragement, there lies encouragement; the world structure dictates the coincidence of opposites. In the midst of discouragement, I am filled with hope; within death itself there is life. In midst of my crying there lies hope. In the mist of national conflict, I see hope and reconciliation. On that note; I am deeply honored for allowing me to visit you, and thank you for lending me your ears. We are related, and we are members of the same family, for we share the canopy known as earth.

BIBLIOGRAPHY

Allport, G.W. Pattern and Growth in Personality. New York: Holt, Rinehart Winston, 1954.

Bennett, J.M. Transformative Training: Designing Programs for Cultural Learning. In Moodian, M.A., editor. *Contemporary Leadership and Intercultural Competence: Understanding and Utilizing Cultures to Build Successful Organizations.* Thousand Oaks, CA: Sage, 2008.

Benaji, Mahzarin R. and Greenwald, A.G. Blind Spot. New York: Bantam Books, 2016.

Bonilla-Silva, Eduardo. Racism Without Racists, 3rd Edition. New York: Rowman & Littlefield Inc., 2010.

DuBois, W.E.B. The Souls of Black Folk, 1903. In *Oxford W.E.B. Du Bois.* Oxford University Press, 2014.

Equiano, Olaudah. The Interesting Narrative of the Life of Olaudah Equiano. 1789.

Fromm, E. The Anatomy of Human Destructiveness. New York: Holt Reinhart & Winston, 1973.

Gernsbacher, Morton Ann. Who's Your Neighbor? Observer, Vol. 19 (10), pp. 5, 29. A Publication of the Association of Psychological Sciences. October, 2006.

Golash-Boza, Tanya Maria. <u>Race and Racisms: A Critical Approach</u>. New York: Oxford University Press, 2015.

<u>Holy Bible New Revised Standard Version, XL Edition</u>. Grand Rapids, Michigan: Zondervan, 1989.

Jones, James M. <u>Prejudice and Racism</u>, 2nd edition. New York: Mc Graw -Hill Companies Inc., 1997.

Jones, James M., Dovido, John F., and Vietze, Deborah L. <u>The Psychology of Diversity: Beyond Prejudice and Racism</u>. Malden, MA: Wiley Blackwell, 2014.

May, Rollo. <u>Contributions of Existential Psychotherapy</u>. In May, R., Angel, E., and Ellenberger, H.F., editors. *Existence: A New Dimension in Psychiatry and Psychotherapy.* New York: Basic Books, 1958.

Neve, Herbert T., editor. <u>Homeward Journey</u>. Trenton, New Jersey: African World Press, Inc., 1994.

Thornton, John. <u>Africa & Africans in the making of the Atlantic World, 1400—1800</u>, 2nd edition. New York: Cambridge University Press, 1998.

Walker, Sheila S., editor. <u>African Roots/American Cultures</u>. Lanham, MD: Rowman & Littlefield, 2001.

Washington, James M., editor. <u>I Have A Dream</u>. San Francisco: Harper, 1986.

Waxman, Sandra R. <u>Racial Awareness and Bias Begin Early: Developmental Entry Points, Challenges, and a Call to Action</u>. *Perspective on Psychological Science. 16 (5),* September, 2021.

Wilkinson, Richard and Pickett, Kate. <u>The Spirit Level: Why More Equal Societies Almost Always Do Better</u>. London: Allen Lane, 2009.